WHOLE CHILD

PARENTING

AGE THREE

Concept by Claudia Sandor

WHOLE CHILD

HEALTH AND CARE

Hygiene
Diet
Routine
Yoga

COGNITIVE
DEVELOPMENT

Problem-solving
Attention
Numbers

PHYSICAL
DEVELOPMENT

Motor skills:
Sensory
Gross
Fine

SOCIAL-EMOTIONAL
DEVELOPMENT

Self-control
Friendship
Feelings

CREATIVE
DEVELOPMENT

Dramatic Play
Dance
Music
Arts

LANGUAGE
DEVELOPMENT

Communication
Speaking
Literacy

WHOLE CHILD:
AGE THREE
Six Areas of Development

WHOLE CHILD

whole \hōl\ **child** \chi-əld\ *compound noun*
1 : a child who is completely developed in all six areas

A **whole child**
grows up to reach
his or her full potential.

A whole child is a **well-rounded** person and lifelong learner.

A whole child is ready to face the world with **confidence**.

A whole child has **self-esteem, knowledge,** and **creativity**.

A whole child will live a **happy** and **fulfilling life**.

Being a successful parent starts with understanding your child.

The Whole Child Parenting Program covers every aspect of a child's cognitive, social-emotional, language, creative, physical, and health and care development.

By using clear examples, color-coded stages, simple and logical steps, age-appropriate materials and toys, developmentally appropriate activities and workbooks, and core parenting books, the Whole Child Program will change the way you think about learning.

Welcome to parenting for the new millenium!

Published by Whole Child Parenting, Inc.
Whole Child Parenting books, activity books, toys, and materials are
available at special discounts when purchased in bulk for premiums
and sales promotions as well as for fundraising or educational use.
For details, please contact us at:
sales@wholechild.co

Whole Child is a registered trademark of Whole Child, LLC
Library of Congress Control Number: 2016905516
ISBN 978-1-944930-03-5

Created by the Whole Child Education Team with:
Early Childhood Education Specialist, Erin Weekes
Book design by Willabel Tong
Art direction by Dan Marmorstein
Editorial direction by Editorial Services of Los Angeles

Visit us on the web at: www.wholechild.co
Email us at: publishing@wholechild.co

Printed in the United States of America.
1 3 5 7 9 10 8 6 4 2

Contents

What Is Whole Child Parenting?

It Is Parenting from Head to Toe

Whole child parenting involves exposing your child to everything he needs to be happy, healthy, well adjusted, smart, and developing right on track. A whole child is a well-rounded person, someone whose innate talents have been developed in every major milestone category and who is ready to face the world with confidence. A whole child has the self-esteem and knowledge to develop his true potential.

Whole child parenting is you doing what you can, with our help, to get him there. The Whole Child Parenting Program is for busy people just like you. With interactive materials that support you at every step, using toys, workbooks, activities, videos, web support, and an app, the Whole Child Parenting Program takes into account the whole child and helps you, the parent or primary caregiver, do what is necessary and best for your child at every stage, every age from infancy to five years old. It helps you parent with a purpose, giving you practical advice and materials that explain the whys and how-tos and goals of each step you take to help your child grow.

Whole child parenting is a process that begins with you. It can be overwhelming to think about the responsibility you have to your three year old in one of the most important years of his life.

Age three is a crucial year because development, in both the body and brain, is happening at a rapid pace. The next 12 months will continue to set the stage for how your child problem solves, communicates, socializes, and thinks for the rest of his life. That is not to say that you won't have amazing experiences with your child when he is three years old. You will have absolutely transformative experiences with your three-year-old child during these next twelve months. You will get to see life from the perspective of a person who is just over three feet tall! And **your presence and influence will always matter the most during this third year of life.** The world is constantly changing; will your child be ready for the global economy years from now? Just by reading this book you are setting yourself along the right path for being the best parent you can be for your three-year-old child.

HOW TO GET ON THE RIGHT TRACK NOW?

Whole Child Parenting: Age Three has six chapters for the six areas of development seen in the column at right. **Each area of development is assigned its own color.**

Each of the six chapters begins with a chart and summary to introduce you to the concepts and terminology in the pages ahead. Within each chapter, **you will also get real-life activities and insights that paint a picture of how your child demonstrates these developmental concepts**

1 Cognitive
Development

2 Social Emotional
Development

3 Language
Development

4 Creative
Development

5 Physical
Development

6 Health and Care

in everyday life. In addition to examples, there are tips and advice for parents and primary caregivers to use to support and guide you as you and your child encounter and master each of the upcoming milestones.

The Whole Child Parenting Program has developed five smart, modern, easy steps to help you raise a happy, thriving child.

> **The Whole Child Parenting Program involves:**
>
> 1. Committing yourself
> 2. Educating yourself
> 3. Creating the right environment
> 4. Using the right materials
> 5. Staying on track

That's it. Five steps to making your experience with your child the most rewarding and productive experience in your life.

STEP ONE: COMMITTING YOURSELF

Let's start with commitment. As a parent you have already taken the huge step of accepting responsibility for the little person in front of you. What is next required might not even be a step that needs articulating for you, but it bears repeating here: **You need to commit quality time to raising your whole child.**

There is no formula or script when it comes to being successful in parenting. Many parents look to doctors, textbooks, and experts for the secrets to parenting success. And while all of these are great sources, none address the whole child. And the whole child needs your attention.

Each child is different and has a different temperament, dif-ferent interests, and a different personality. As a parent, you are also different. Every parent has different values that come from being a part of different cultures, socioeconomic classes, education levels, religions, and family sizes. The best way to be successful in parenting is to be involved with your child. By being involved and communicating with your child, you are better able to support her and her needs.

Many wonder what the real measures and outcomes of good parenting are. It does not involve your child having a high IQ, being talented in sports, or making a lot of money. Good parenting results in raising a child who grows up to give back to society, is independent, has a good work ethic, gets along well with others, and understands her identity and self-worth.

When it comes to measuring your success as a parent, it is important to look at the quality of the relationship you have with your child and not how effectively you can control your child. Just because your child listens and follows the rules does not mean she understands or respects them; it just means she is obedient.

The quality of your relation-ship has to do with your in-volvement and communication with your child. Know what guidelines are appropriate to set for your child, and explain them in a way that shows why these rules are necessary and important. As a parent, you need to meet your child's needs and help her feel respected. This can be done by explaining the reasons behind rules and discussing your child's feelings and opinions.

When your child feels like she is a valued member of the family and the community, she will then develop the confidence needed to begin moving toward being independent and making her own decisions.

Parents who are uninvolved with their children tend to make their children feel ignored and unvalued. At the same time, parents who are overly controlling and establish strict rules over all avenues of their children's lives tend to make their children feel stressed and have low self-esteem. It is important to find the middle ground between control-ling your child and overlooking your child.

Your child is born naturally impul-sive, immature, and ambitious, and she looks to you for guidance and support. This is why it is important to **make sure you communicate clear guidelines and expec-tations** for your child to alleviate stress and misunderstandings.

THE FOUR STYLES OF PARENTING

Whole Child Parenting: Age Three combines research, expert advice, and firsthand experience. In the past few decades, early childhood education has grown exponentially.

In the late 1950s, psychologist Erik Erikson organized development from birth to death into eight stages; according to Erikson, a person cannot successfully excel in the next stage of life without first completing the stage before.

Looking specifically at the first three stages, which cover ages birth to five, we see that a person's success lies first in his relationship with his parents. **Stage 1,** covering ages birth to two years old, focuses on a child's ability to develop **trust** with his parents. From there, children move on to **Stage 2** (for ages two to four years old), when the child is developing autonomy. **Autonomy** is your child's sense of self as an individual. Your child develops a sense of self by exploring the en-vironment, learning about his own interests, and testing his limits. Moving forward to **Stage 3** (ages four to five years old), your child is **finding his purpose and place** within the family.

In the last 40 years, developmental psychologists have established **four styles of parenting.** The best par-enting style is a combination of these four parenting styles—one in which you approach different situations with different solutions and always communicate with your child.

Authoritarian Parenting

The authoritarian parenting style can best be described as strict. Authoritarian parents tend to set rules that result in rewards or punishment if they are not followed. Rules are not explained and usually follow a reasoning of "because I said so." **These parents usually set high demands and expect obedience** but are not very responsive to their children. Children who grow up under the authoritarian parenting style tend to be obedient and usually well performing in school but socially exhibit signs of shame, low self-esteem, and lowered happiness levels.

Authoritative Parenting

The authoritative parenting style establishes rules and guidelines for children instead of just demands. Authoritative parents are more nurturing and forgiving, rather than simply punishing. They are responsive to their children and willing to listen and answer questions.

An important quality of authoritative parents is that they create clear standards for their children and adjust those standards based on their children's conduct.

Children who grow up under the authoritative parenting style tend to be capable and successful at learning new things. Socially and emotionally,

they feel accepted and tend to be happy.

Permissive Parenting

The permissive parenting style is one that has few demands or guidelines. Parents tend to have low expectations for their children's maturity and abilities. **Permissive parents are more lenient with rules, preferring to avoid confrontation.**

This parenting style is usually nurturing and communicative but leaves children looking at their parent as more of a friend. Children who grow up under the permissive parenting style tend to often have poor self-regulation skills and may experience problems with authority and have trouble in school.

Uninvolved Parenting

The uninvolved parenting style is one with even fewer demands as well as little communication and responsiveness. Uninvolved parents fulfill their children's basic needs but tend to be detached and unavailable for their children in all other areas.

Children who grow up under the uninvolved parenting style tend to have low self-esteem, a hard time regulating their emotions, and a hard time making friends.

Your child's personality and temperament play a major role in how you choose your parenting style. Research shows correlations between parenting styles and their impact on children. There is also evidence showing other factors, such as a child's personality and the outside environment, playing a role as well. Your larger environment—such as culture, religion, socio-economic class, and family style—can also affect how your child reacts to your parenting. School, friends, and personality play a significant role in how your child responds to your parenting style.

It is important to be consistent with your parenting style, especially when it comes to discipline and setting expectations for your child. Besides taking into account her environment, think about other people in your child's life, such as your spouse or partner or caregiver. Take time to talk to each other about parenting styles and how you will work together when raising your child. Talk about what you both value as important and how you were each raised; this is important for keeping your parenting style consistent.

At the end of the day, you need to remember to be present and realistic. **Be present both physically and mentally in order to be responsive to your child's needs.** Be realistic in your expectations and the guidelines you set for your child.

Committing quality time as a parent, whichever parenting style(s) you choose, is the single most important factor in your child's healthy development.

STEP TWO: EDUCATING YOURSELF

Addressing the whole child means knowing about the general developmental milestones your child will experience at each age. Milestones define peak stages of accomplishment when your child achieves the end of one stage before moving on to the next. **Milestones are exciting, because when a child reaches one you get to see how far she has come.** And you get to look forward to the next amazing stage your whole child will go through.

But how can you be aware of milestones without knowing the specific developmental categories the stages occur in? How can you have realistic expectations about what is age appropriate and what your whole child should or should not be doing? *Whole Child Parenting: Age Three* lays out six major developmental areas of your child's growth and follows them through this year of your child's development.

Cognitive development

The first area of development is cognitive development. Cognitive development refers to the process of learning and the growth of intelligence and other mental capabilities, such as memory, reasoning, problem solving, and thinking. Memory and problem solving play a large role in your child's ability to engage in science, mathematical thinking, and logic.

Your involvement strengthens your child's cognitive abilities over these next years and plays a significant role in her school readiness and how she will learn and retain information later in life. At birth, your child's brain is only a quarter of the size of an adult brain; by age five, it has grown to be close to the same size and volume as yours.

Take advantage of these first five years to set the path and exercise the brain to its fullest potential. The Whole Child Parenting Program will very clearly define the stages of cognitive development and will help you be involved in your child's growth in this area.

Social-emotional development

Social-emotional skills reflect how effectively your child is able to interact in social settings. In order to interact well he must develop positive relationships. He must learn to recognize and regulate his emotions and reactions while communicating his feelings.

For young children, social-emotional skills provide a pivotal foundation upon which are built a range of other skills that are necessary in preschool as well as on play dates. Development in this category will help to determine how well your child succeeds with peer interaction throughout his life.

In order to interact well with others your child must develop positive relationships with others. He must also effectively coordinate his actions with communicating his feelings. As well, he must learn to recognize and regulate his emotions and reactions in many different social settings.

Your child needs to have good self-regulatory skills (i.e. the ability to calm himself down), keen emotional understanding (i.e. learning with help what made him feel the way he does), and growing communication skills such as naming how he feels and dealing with those feelings.

Language development

Language development is how your child communicates, from basic sounds and gestures to the use of pictures in books and words for speaking. As she ages your child will be communicating more than her emotions and needs. She will begin to tell stories, ask questions, and describe people and objects.

Your child will use memory to remember words and past events when telling stories. At an early age, your child's memory will also play a role in symbolic play when she uses props and objects as symbols to represent her ideas. These symbols will later translate to letter recognition and emerging literacy.

The Whole Child Parenting Program identifies how to use sign language to support early literacy skills, and we also include signs in supplemental and supportive materials in the program. Sign language for communication plays a role in your child's social-emotional development because it makes her better able to convey her emotions and needs when she is largely preverbal.

Creative development

Creative development involves how your child uses music, art, movement, and dramatic play to express himself and build imaginative thinking. When doing art, let your child make a mess and indulge in all the different textures and materials you provide. Make a paintbrush or other tools available to your child and then let him explore the paint with his hands. **Creative development plays a big role in your child's physical development as well.** Music and movement build your child's gross motor skills (big muscles) by allowing your child to test balance and large body movements. Visual art builds your child's fine motor skills (small muscles) by allowing him to explore materials such as scissors, paintbrushes, and crayons.

Creative development can be used as an avenue for social-emotional development. Through art and dramatic play, your child can express and act out feelings, model behavior, or work through emotions.

Through activities, examples, and tips, *Whole Child Parenting: Age Three* shows how important creative development can be to your child's other areas of development as well.

Physical development

Physical development refers to your child's control over fine motor skills (small muscle movements of fingers, toes, and wrists) and gross motor skills (bigger movements that use the large muscles in the arms, legs, and torso). Between birth and five years old, your child's body and motor abilities make great strides.

Physical development has a lot to do with your child's self-esteem and sense of trust. Your child is more willing to test her physical skills of throwing, kicking, and balancing when she feels comfortable and confident within her environment.

Physical development is important because it plays a large role in children developing independence and self-help skills. Getting dressed, feeding themselves, and cleaning up are all skills that involve both fine and gross motor skills, which, when combined, develop sensory motor skills.

The Whole Child Parenting Program explains how your child's physical changes correlate with the development of motor abilities and overall physical growth and development.

Health and care

This section discusses safety, grooming, self-help, and the health of your child. As your child grows older, he will be more independent with his hygiene, from small achievements like brushing his own teeth to bigger accomplishments like potty training.

As he goes through each developmental stage, your child's body is changing and growing at a swift pace. He is growing taller, sprouting new teeth, and becoming more active, which will reflect in changes in his diet each year.

Whole child parenting also involves using yoga. Yoga is a great resource in which to engage your child from infancy through age four and beyond. Not only does it allow your child to explore his balance, but it also strengthens his social-emotional development by helping him find an avenue to calm himself. Yoga can also provide a bonding experience for parent and child.

Reaching Milestones

An important and exciting addition to our exploration of the six developmental categories is the Reaching Milestones section we provide at the end of the book. This assessment list will allow you to see everything your child should be doing and accomplishing developmentally around that age. Milestone assessments provide an exciting reflection of all that you are doing to support your whole child.

STEP THREE: CREATING THE RIGHT ENVIRONMENT

Now that you have committed your time and started educating yourself, it is time to follow through by setting up the right environment. Setting up an environment where your whole child will thrive plays a large role in all six areas of their development.

The importance of play

We are in a day and age in which there is an abundance of technology and information available to us. It is hard to remember a time when an answer to a question wasn't a mouse click away or we couldn't watch a video about how to fix something.

Technology has made our lives so much easier over the years, but that is not the case when it comes to our little ones. Young children need to have the opportunity to make their own connections and discoveries within their environment. Children between the ages of birth and three learn the most through play.

When setting up an environment that fosters **free play**, it is important to have child-sized furniture as well as incorporate baskets and trays for storing toys. Child-sized furniture and organizational materials such as bins and trays for different categories of toys help your child build independence and self-help skills. Being able to pick what he wants to play with from the shelf or bin will build upon your child's personal interests.

Just because your child is more in control of what activity and materials he is exploring in free play does not mean that you do not need to be involved in free play with your child. Setting up learning and play environments and making learning materials available is just part of encouraging free play. When watching your child explore materials in free play, it is important to interact with him.

The main aspect to remember about free play is that your child's interests guide it.

Structured play is also an important type of play and can help foster and build specific skills. Structured play differs from free play based on the fact that you are planning the activity and materials in which your child is engaging. You are leading the way with a specific activity that has a specific goal. Examples of structured activities can be doing a science experiment with your child or sorting different colored blocks. It is important to have both a combination of structured and free play activities available for your child.

Indoor environments

Incorporating child-sized furniture as well as baskets and trays for storing toys helps your child build independence and self-help skills.

Trays and baskets allow you to provide more manipulatives (age appropriate toys that foster growth) for your child and make it easier for your child to help care for and clean her environment. **When furniture and materials are at your child's eye level, she is able to have better control of her physical movements and be more aware of her environment.**

When setting up an environment that is beneficial for your child's language skills, it is important to have age-appropriate books available. Your child's interest in books both while reading with you as well as pretending to read on her own helps her relate words to pictures. Take your child's language learning to the next level and place labels like TABLE on your kitchen table. Your child will start making the connection between words and objects.

When doing art, let your child get messy and indulge in all the different textures and materials you provide. Investing in an easel, putting down a tarp, providing a smock, or buying washable paint can help you make your indoor environment fit for creative exploration. Having some paper and crayons out on a table that is child-sized makes expressing herself and her ideas easy. She can use the crayons to express herself creatively and create symbols that depict her feelings or needs.

Besides art materials, your child can express her thoughts and feelings through dramatic play by modeling roles and situations when dressing up or using props. Having a mirror in your child's room allows her to explore her self-concept skills. You will find your child making different faces in the mirror or watching herself stack blocks. Having a mirror that is at your child's eye level builds her self-concept by developing a better understanding of herself as an individual who has her own interests and ideas. Don't overwhelm your child with too many choices or structured activities, but instead follow your child's needs and interests to help encourage independence.

Your commitment to your child is very important when it comes to building attention span and memory skills. Having a rug or a chair that is child-sized will make your child more comfortable and thus want to spend longer on an activity. Your child's attention span is a cognitive skill, and it grows as your child grows older.

The Whole Child Parenting Program provides you with all the guidelines, furniture, educational books, activities, supplies, and toys for your whole child's stimulating environment.

Outdoor environments

Environments where your child can engage in free play allow him to develop self-identity and develop his own interests. He is able to learn more about himself by testing his cognitive and physical limits. There aren't always many opportunities for your child to fully engage in free play at home, which is why outdoor environments provide beneficial play spaces for your child.

By its nature, play is flexible, changeable, and multifaceted, so your child's play environment should reflect those criteria as well. Play is a core and vital component of how young children learn. Structured and unstructured play provide health benefits by allowing your child to be physically active as well as engaging in problem-solving and creative exploration.

Outdoor environments provide space and opportunities for structured activities that help children learn to communicate and work together, while unstructured activities in large, open areas help your child push the limits and take risks. Your child can make a mess, climb, shout, jump, and run as fast as he wants in open spaces. He can fully express himself and explore his body's movements. From this, your child will develop a sense of competence and confidence in his own physical abilities.

Large, open areas provide opportunities for your child to be creative and use his imagination. He can make connections and witness vivid colors, patterns, and textures in an outdoor environment.

Without material items, media, or structured rules, children can create their own games, engage in dramatic play, and entertain themselves through the use of their mighty imagination. Nature provides an abundance of science and math opportunities that your child can explore and manipulate. Problem solving, learning cause and effect, and investigating use all of your child's senses. Your child will be exposed to nature and its elements and make connections by witnessing weather, ecology, growth, and natural life cycles. He can explore what happens when he throws a rock in a pond, adds water to dirt or sand, or watches snow melt.

It is not always easy to find a safe outdoor environment for your child. For families in the city, it may mean you need to travel a little farther, but the benefits are worth it. Outdoor environments can actually be considered cleaner than indoor environments, especially when it comes to germs.

By being in a large space with richly fresh air, germs and infectious agents are spread out. Indoor spaces tend to be more enclosed, which leaves bacteria to sit on surfaces and linger. Overall, the benefits of outdoor environments are enormous, and you need to take advantage of them.

How you set up your child's indoor and outdoor environments plays a large role in how he learns and develops. It is important to remember that you are a part of his environment and **in order for your child to thrive, he needs both a rich learning environment and your involvement.**

STEP FOUR: USING THE RIGHT MATERIALS

As parents, we frequently buy and invest in products and toys that are not age appropriate and serve no purpose developmentally, which is why The Whole Child Parenting Program has created developmentally appropriate tools and materials for the whole child that are both fun and educational.

When starting the Whole Child Parenting Program from infancy, you are able to build and adjust your child's environment and learning materials as she grows older. Many materials, such as toys and furniture, are able to grow with your child from infancy to kindergarten. Other materials, such as Whole Child Parenting activity books, toys, and parent resources, assist you with staying on track with your child's development while also helping you plan and measure your time and commitment to your child. The Whole Child Parenting Program is here to walk with you through these first five years.

A variety and quantity of materials are needed to accommodate young children's short attention spans. Children learn through concrete activities, and parents must be able to provide activities for both their physical, active needs and calm, quiet needs.

Having the right environment with both active and quiet play can help your child's social-emotional development by encouraging self-regulating skills. Having a quiet area to go to when your child feels overstimulated or needs a break is just as essential as having a safe area for her to be active and test her physical and creative limits.

A variety of materials is required to stimulate the development of each age group. Some materials may fit into one or more categories; for example, an art activity can also serve as a fine motor exercise, and dramatic play can also act as a social-emotional tool.

It is important to remember that in order for your child to be able to explore and manipulate materials, she needs to have the materials made easily available to her at all times of the day. Setting up the right environment and investing in furniture that is both safe and easily accessible will play an important role in supporting your child's development.

STEP FIVE: STAYING ON TRACK

Once you have set up your environment, the Whole Child Parenting Program makes staying on track easier by providing you with activity books, toys, and learning materials. Consistency and routine play a big role in your whole child's development, so it is up to you to follow through and use these materials with your child.

Five years may seem far away, but time always has a way of sneaking up on us. In the blink of an eye, your child will be five years old and boarding the bus for school. This is a big milestone in your child's life, but you will be confident your child is ready for school because the Whole Child Parenting Program has helped you stay on track with your child's development. Your child is leaving for school a confident, happy, healthy learner.

In the end, all we want for our children is for them to be happy and confident because happiness and confidence set your child on the road to success. The Whole Child Parenting Program is here to get you to that point so you can take a deep breath and know your child is ready to face the world.

Through our *Whole Child Parenting: Age Three* book, educational materials, and workbooks, tips, and activities, apps, videos, and web support, you will have the tools to build a relationship with your child that allows him to confidently express himself through his creative and social-emotional skills, which in turn help him build his cognitive, language, and physical skills. You want your child to be healthy, happy, and complete, developing at or ahead of the curve. The Whole Child Parenting Program was developed for you, the committed and caring parent.

three >

Milestones for a Three Year Old

COGNITIVE  1

- Names some colors
- Understands the concept of counting
- Recognizes some numbers and letters
- Develops a sense of time

SOCIAL-EMOTIONAL  2

- Acts more independent
- Plays with other children
- Develops empathy for others

LANGUAGE 3

- Speaks in five- to six-word sentences
- Tells stories
- Asks questions

CREATIVE 4

- Draws a person with two to four body parts
- Engages in pretend play with peers

PHYSICAL 5

- Moves forward and backward
- Stands on one foot for five seconds
- Kicks ball forward
- Copies and traces shapes

HEALTH AND CARE  6

- Gains independence with brushing teeth
- Develops daily routines
- Exhibits preschool readiness

three

At three years old, children have better control of their emotions and begin problem solving and thinking of solutions to their problems instead of acting out by hitting or screaming. They are developing a better sense of time and a clearer understanding of their daily routine. Because of this, three year olds are able to become more independent with personal care routines such as dressing and undressing themselves and washing their own hands. Three is a big year.

1. Cognitive Development

> **Cognitive development skills enable your child to process information, reason through problems, and develop language and memory.**

Cognitive development is the building of thinking methods, which includes how your child will remember, problem solve, and make decisions from now and into adulthood.

Three year olds are able to sit and focus for longer periods of time, which enables them to take in more information. They also ask a lot of questions and are very inquisitive.

During cognitive development, children will grasp language, persevere through problems (like puzzles), ask a lot of questions (about things they see or hear), and remember past and upcoming events.

Remember, your child will develop at his own pace; however, there are still typical cognitive goals he must achieve during this age in order to be developing on track.

The following chart provides you with an image that walks you through the stages of your child's intellectual development.

Understanding these areas of cognitive development will help you learn how your child thinks, how to support learning, and how to teach new skills.

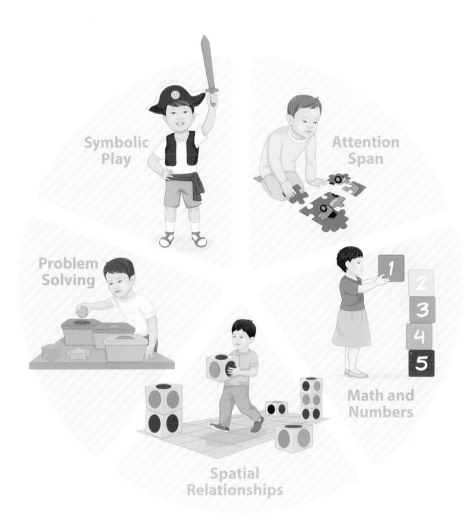

WHOLE CHILD: AGE THREE
Cognitive
Development Components

Attention Span >
Stimulate My Brain

Attention span refers to the amount of time your child is able to concentrate on or focus on a single activity.

Supporting the development of your child's attention skills, along with his self-regulation skills, will form his foundation for learning. Strong attention skills will set the stage for your child to have success in everything from learning math to his social relationships. In addition, strong attention skills can help your child learn to read before age five, have improved memory, and achieve a host of other amazing milestones.

ACTIVITY

Gabe wants to have a friend over for a play date. Mom agrees to have one friend come over. Mom says to Gabe, "Your friend is coming over. What should we do?" Gabe says, "A dance party! We love to dance. Look at me move." Mom thinks for a moment and says, "Okay! Dance party it is. You have to help me get things ready." Gabe says, "I'll get the music!" Gabe goes to his parents' room and grabs Mom's guitar for her. "Here you go, Mom!"

Gabe's friend arrives with her mom, and they go downstairs to have fun. In the beginning the children are talking and playing. Gabe's mom says, "It's time for a dance party!" Gabe and his friend scream "Yeah!" and jump up and down.

Mom tells the children, "For the first part of our dance party you can dance until the music stops. When the music stops you should stop dancing." Mom begins to play her guitar. After a few short minutes she stops and starts it again. After doing this several times,

Gabe's mom says, "Now I want you to listen for me to strum the guitar fast. When you hear me stop you should stop dancing and listen." Gabe and his friend dance and stop for 30 seconds then dance again until they are all danced out. Gabe's friend says, "That was so fun, Gabe! Can I come to your house again?"

INSIGHT

Through this activity Mom gives the children an opportunity to practice attention skills, especially when she asks them to listen for the guitar playing. Mom also helps the children develop attention skills because this activity allows both children to actively participate as opposed to passively listen during the entire activity.

Help build attention span

1. Speak a language of attention—Attention is a set of three skills: focus, awareness, and a set of mental skills that helps your child get things done, e.g. planning and decision making. Play Spot the Letter on a car ride. As you drive, call out a letter for your child to spot along the way, choosing easy to see objects like a stop sign for the letter S.

2. Focus on one another—A meeting of the minds comes from focusing on something together. Set the table for dinner together with your child.

3. White space, also known as uninterrupted time—Put an end to distractions to support developing attention skills in your child and provide a space for him to focus. Limit TV time, video games, and other electronics.

4. Eat mindfully—You may have noticed we are a society that eats on the run. Take time to stop and eat as a family, talking together about the food you are eating, how it smells, looks, and tastes.

Typically, your child will have the most difficulty with paying attention during activities that involve sitting and listening. This is normal behavior, and it occurs because at this age your child will become bored very easily and needs a variety of activities to stimulate his whole brain.

Your child's left side of the brain, which deals directly with logic, language, critical thinking, numbers, and reasoning can be referred to as the "seat of learning;" it is eager to take on new information. Provide lots of simple brain-stimulating activities so that your child can learn and develop his attention span.

Your three year old has a limited attention span. Build up attention skills over time. Do an activity for a minute, and then later do the same activity for a few minutes longer.

Over the next week, do at least two of the listed activities in the box to the left with your child. Start doing the activity every three days and then build up to every day. Building your child's attention span takes time and encouragement, and development must continue well into adolescence.

The quantity, quality, and consistency of stimulation you provide through experiences with your child will play a part in the developing structure of his brain and its capacity. By strengthening your child's brain, you will improve his ability to focus and pay attention to any task that he becomes involved in.

Remember, the Whole Child Parenting Program

offers appropriate developmental products and monthly activity books that walk you through supporting your child's skills. Using these in conjunction with the recommended age-appropriate room materials ensures faster development.

Math and Numbers >
I Spy with My Eyes

Math and number awareness involves your child counting, recognizing numbers and patterns, learning one-to-one correspondence, sorting, and classifying.

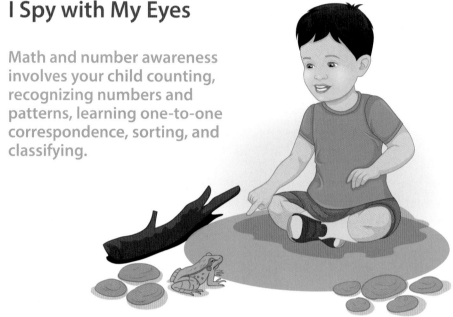

ACTIVITY

Adam is on the floor of his bedroom playing with a variety of toys he has taken out of his toy box. He discovers a few rocks of different sizes, a plastic frog, and a plastic tree branch.

Mom comes in his bedroom and says, "Adam, you're so quiet. What do you have?" He replies, "Look at all this stuff I found in my toy chest!" Mom replies, "Oh, wow! Look at this rock. It has all of these light colored lines on it." "Let me see," says Adam.

Mom asks, "Why don't we see how many other rocks we can find that look just like this rock here and count them?"

INSIGHT

Adam's experience playing with a collection of rocks is a powerful math experience. As he learns to match the rocks he is learning concepts of math through play and hands-on experience. Mom supports her son by asking him to pay attention, notice how the rocks are the same, and group them in like categories. Mom also extends the learning experience by the two of them counting out how many rocks they have that look the same. Using simple materials and bonding together creates a meaningful math experience.

Mathematical thinking involves seeing how your child uses his brain to play with the concepts of parts and wholes and his ability to see math in everyday life.

Mathematical thinking is important for three reasons: it is a necessary skill to master in your child's schooling experience; it is a way of learning mathematics itself; and it helps your child in solving problems later in life.

One of the best ways to build early mathematical thinking skills in your child is to make numbers and math concepts fun and relatable to the everyday experiences he has. This will increase his desire to learn more and have an appreciation for math in the future.

Early math concepts appropriate for your child include shape sorting, matching games (putting one part with another part), color sorting, and simply playing with collections of things (seeing math in everyday life).

In this next example, you get a glimpse of how Maria is on her way to becoming a mathematician by interacting with ants. Learning about numbers is one of the first steps to your child becoming a mathematical thinker. She will become a mathematician through counting, number recognition, and one-to-one correspondence activities.

ACTIVITY

Maria is in her backyard kicking around a new ball Mom just bought her, when she accidentally kicks the ball in the area of the garbage cans. Maria runs over to get the ball and stops in her tracks, staring down at the ground. There are a bunch of ants in a line.

Maria runs inside to tell her dad. "Dad, come see the ants!" Maria grabs Dad's hand and heads toward the backyard. While she is walking with her dad, she begins to sing. "The ants go marching one by one, hurrah, hurrah. The ants go marching two by two, hurrah, hurrah."

Maria bends down to look at the ants on the ground and pulls Dad down with her. She tries to count the ants but they are just too small and numerous to count.

INSIGHT

Even though Maria cannot point to and count each ant on the ground, she is singing about numbers and uses simple counting while she sings the song and marches. This is counting using a **math rhyme**. It is simple and fun and happens through an everyday experience. You see how fun math can be for your child, and you have the distinct pleasure of being a part of the process!

Spatial Relationships >
The Genius of Seeing

Spatial relationships are related to how your child can maintain her body in connection to the surrounding environment when she is at rest and during movement.

ACTIVITY

Aubrey and her parents have just come back from the theater. Aubrey is so excited to get into the house because Grandpa is back from his fishing trip. She jumps out of the car and runs into the house and into the kitchen. Aubrey does not notice that the kitchen chair by the wall is going to be in her way and runs right into it, stubbing her toe.

INSIGHT

Aubrey is unable to navigate and avoid the contact with the chair either because she doesn't see it, or because she doesn't realize just how big she is and that she cannot fit in between the chair and the wall without moving the movable object. Aubrey's spatial relationships skills are still developing.

Understanding spatial relationships is a required skill for your child to have as she learns to navigate through life. When your child has the ability to understand her position (where the body is) in relation to things around her, then she can avoid obstacles. Your child's brain has to consistently think about where everything is, especially her own body.

Spatial relationship skills will continue to develop naturally over time as you support your child's skill building. Your child will also increase this skill through making more observations of where things are in her environment. Help her out by making obstacle courses at home with sheets and chairs. Also play Hide and Seek with your child; you'll both have a good time.

Problem Solving >
Independent Thinking

Problem solving refers to your child's ability to use the knowledge and information she has already acquired to find answers to difficult or complicated issues that are occurring now.

ACTIVITY

Three-year-old Elizabeth is trying to stack all of the blocks she got from her birthday, but they keep falling over. She wants to make a tower that is taller than she is. She remembers watching her older brother make a really tall tower yesterday. Fascinated with the idea of doing the same things her brother does, Elizabeth decides to solve her problem by imitating what she saw her brother do.

Elizabeth begins by putting the larger block on the bottom, and then she continues by stacking the blocks one on top of the other. She makes sure that the blocks are a bit staggered as opposed to lined up the same exact way. She smiles and says, "It's working, they are not falling over!"

INSIGHT

Through this simple experience Elizabeth finds a solution to her problem by remembering back to something she has seen her brother do, and then applying her problem-solving skills to come up with a solution to keep the blocks from falling over. When parents or siblings see a child engage in problem solving skills, it is very important to provide encouragement and praise for the efforts they are making to think independently and make decisions for themselves when and where appropriate.

Every day your child takes in new information and then tests that new information. Your child's ability to acquire this information and store it for later problem solving is dependent on the support and nurturing you provide through these experiences. The information she already knows enables her to use a variety of approaches to solve problems. Even if she fails the first time, she will try one or even two different strategies before she begins

---

Many problem-solving skills are important for brain development. Here's how you can nurture the development of problem-solving skills:

1. Open the window for learning opportunities by creating hands-on problem-solving experiences with learning toys and materials or even everyday household items.

2. Be responsive to your child's signals for support or attention; this builds trust.

3. Create a safe environment, allow mistakes to be made, and reduce stress.

4. Give time each day to practicing songs and stories and looking at books with words.

5. Always remember to give opportunities for your child to work above her current abilities with help from you (toss a ball and expand how far you toss over time).

to get overwhelmed and frustrated.

You will notice that your child is learning from her mistakes and using the feedback given to her when you see how she changes her techniques to solve the next problem. Your child's ability to use trial and error thinking skills—by touching and doing—is one of the most important cognitive developments during this age.

Encouraging independence promotes problem-solving abilities. When your child has a "problem," such as a toy that won't make that special noise, she becomes motivated to figure out why. Motivation drives children's problem-solving skills.

Remember you must be present and provide support to your child when needed. If she becomes too overwhelmed with trying to find a solution to a problem, she will give up and the learning opportunity will be lost. Problem-solving skills are tools that your child will use for the rest of her life.

Learning continues throughout your child's life. But there are "prime times" or "windows of opportunity" when the brain is a super sponge, absorbing new information each day. Now is one of those prime times!

ACTIVITY

 Justin is playing with his new puzzle on the basement floor of his house. He is having a hard time trying to fit one of the puzzle pieces into the puzzle board. After turning the piece in several directions (up then down, right then left), Justin starts huffing loudly and says, "I can't." Dad hears Justin and comes over onto the floor next to him. Dad asks, "What's wrong? Can I help you?" When Justin says yes, Dad gives him some clues that will help him find where to place the puzzle piece.

INSIGHT

Here we see that Dad supports Justin before he becomes too frustrated. Dad also asks if he wants support instead of jumping right in. This shows that he acknowledges his son's own efforts, which in turn builds Justin's self-esteem.

Teach problem solving to your child slowly, patiently, and consistently! Learning is a process that happens over time.

Symbolic Play >
Thinking

Symbolic play is
a type of thinking
in which symbols
or internal images
(images in your
child's mind) are
used to represent
objects, persons,
and events that
are not present.

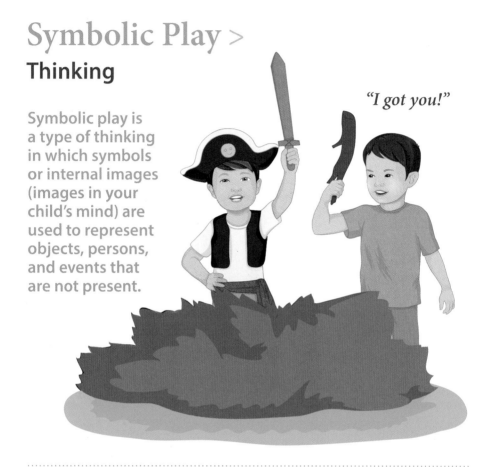

"I got you!"

ACTIVITY

 Kieran's next-door neighbor comes over for a play date with his pirate hat and sword. The two boys go outside in the backyard; Kieran finds a medium length stick on the ground and together the boys begin to play swords. Going back and forth they trade shouts, "I got you!" "No, I got you!" Kieran and his friend transform themselves into pirates fighting for treasure.

INSIGHT

Kieran finds an object to represent a sword and thus uses symbolic thinking to play with his neighbor. A parent can provide support by extending the play experience. Give the child unusual materials to play with, perhaps items that are not usually used for playing, like a frying pan for a shield or a bandana for an eye patch.

You can see symbolic thought occurring in your child's play, especially during times when he is engaged in social interactions.

Symbolic thinking involves symbols or internal images used to represent objects. When we provide three year olds with socio-dramatic play opportunities, we must also include materials (e.g. a box, broom, empty cans) to play with. By doing so you encourage your child to use his symbolic thinking skills. These materials allow your child to use objects to stand for things that are completely different, thus supporting symbolic thought.

Your child puts a lot of thought into a symbolic play event. He has to think about what he wants to be, think about what objects he wants to use to transform himself, and think about how to be or do something new. It requires a lot of imagination and memory.

Memory goes hand in hand with symbolic play because in order for your child to imitate the behavior of what he sees in his mind, he must store and later retrieve information about the behavior from his memory. As your child grows, his ability to store more information over a period of time (weeks and months) and pull from his memory for later use will increase. This will then make his symbolic play more complex and longer in duration. In a few years you can sign him up for a play at school or a theater class.

Symbolic play provides a great example of your child integrating experiences from her past into her present to plan for her future.

2. Social-Emotional Development

> **During the preschool years, social-emotional development is about socialization, which is the process by which your child learns values and behaviors accepted by society.**

Social-emotional development is also about becoming a confident person who has a sense of self and can take responsibility for himself. Children who develop the skills to make and keep a friend, to cooperate with others, and to participate in groups are more likely to adjust to and be successful in school.

WHOLE CHILD: AGE THREE
Social-Emotional
Development Components

Your child's social-emotional development provides him with a sense of who he is in the world, how he deals with stress, and also helps him form relationships with others. The development of these skills is what stimulates him to communicate with others, resolve conflicts, gain confidence, and reach personal goals. Social skills serve people well throughout their lives as does emotional intelligence.

1. Social Development

Your child likes to be around other children his age. He will play alongside other children, using toys and playing games. Children learn to understand how to take turns and can now use words to express themselves in social settings.

2. Emotional Development

Emotional development at this age is observed as your child becomes strong-willed and disagreeable. He may at times become emotionally insecure and anxious. He may also be picky and hard to please. This emotional instability is due to his gaining more independence.

3. Self-Regulation

Self-regulation refers to your child's ability to regulate his thinking, emotions, and behavior. Self-regulation is critical for school and relationship success.

4. Self-Awareness

Children this age are excited about what they would like to become; they engage in many different imaginative activities, which enables them to discover themselves. They discover what type of athlete, musician, peer, and friend they really are.

At age three your child can express empathy as part of her toolbox of social-emotional skills.

Remember, the Whole Child Parenting Program offers appropriate developmental products and monthly activity books that walk you through supporting your child's skills. Using these in conjunction with the recommended age-appropriate room materials ensures faster development.

Social Development >
Let's Talk About You and Me

Empathy involves your child's ability to put herself into another person's shoes and to experience something as that other person would.

ACTIVITY

 Mina is sitting on the ground waiting for her friends Tegan and Gia at the park, while the moms watch nearby. The two girls began to whisper in each other's ear about who has the best dress on. Tegan turns to Gia and whispers, "My dress is better than Mina's!" Mina drops her head and folds her hands. Mina starts to cry. Gia walks over to Mina and begins to comfort her by patting her on the back. Gia asks, "Mina, are you okay? I'm sad you're crying. I'll get my mom."

INSIGHT

Gia is showing empathy toward Mina by asking if she is okay and even offering to get support so that her friend can feel better. When Gia says she is sad that Mina is crying it is her way of putting herself in Mina's shoes. This is a newer skill for a three year old. Gia's social skills have developed over time.

At age three, your child takes a huge leap into the world of socialization. When children this age are exposed to social opportunities, they will most naturally gravitate toward social play. **It is the role of the parent and caregivers to help "coach" their child through social interactions when needed.** Parents and adults need to give their child the words to join into play and give her options about how to resolve conflicts.

Starting to learn these skills now will help promote self-confidence in your child and make her feel positive about playing with other children. During this time, your child will also start developing a sense of humor and the ability to show empathy for others.

When your child was younger she would look to you for guidance about how to deal with social situations with friends. **As children get older, they become more confident and independent and less dependent on others to work through social events.**

Help your child understand empathy for others by modeling empathy and pointing out situations that call for empathy. If you and your child see someone getting hurt on TV, talk with your child about how that person must feel. Read books about characters showing empathy and helping to find solutions for another character's problem.

And encourage your child to interact with family members, peers, caregivers, and teachers.

Emotional Development >
Calm, Cool, Collected

Social-emotional wellness involves developing the ability to experience and control emotions, form secure and positive relationships, and explore and learn in all areas of your child's environment (family, community, and culture).

Reading your child's emotional cues will help her identify her emotions. Also model for her the behavior for dealing with the emotion so she can store that information and use it the next time a similar situation arises or the feeling is experienced again.

Your child mirrors your own expressions and gestures. It is important to always model and provide emotional support for your child. Social-emotional maturity is a necessary skill to have in social settings, and each age has its milestones in this category.

ACTIVITY

Aunt Lisa comes over to see Helen's new baby brother. Helen is upset that she has not come to see only her. Mom sees Helen with her arms crossed and sitting on the couch. Mom asks, "Helen, are you sad?" Helen nods. Mom says, "Helen, it's okay. I will sit with you, and we can ask Aunt Lisa to bring your baby brother over while we all sit together." Mom comforts Helen with a hug and a kiss. As they wait for Aunt Lisa they sit together on the couch having some special togetherness time.

INSIGHT

In this situation Mom takes the time to identify to Helen how she is feeling, then she provides comfort to her and brings her into the experience so she does not feel replaced in everyone's affections by her baby brother. This is also very important to do since Helen is feeling excluded from the situation, and feeling left out brings feelings of sadness and isolation.

Three year olds form relationships and learn to express their feelings during play experiences with others as the children work toward a common goal and communicate how they feel.

Relationships play a key role in cultivating your child's social-emotional well-being, providing a sense of stability and belonging, and allowing the child to make the most of learning opportunities. Social relationships between children also allow the child to learn appropriate ways to express herself when interacting with others.

Your child's emotional development requires your support by helping her have a positive self-image. When your child accomplishes a physical feat or deals with an emotion in a positive manner, praise her. **A "good job!" goes a long way in reinforcing appropriate social-emotional reactions.** You will keep coaching and encouraging your child's emotional development into her adolescent years.

Self-Regulation >
Control

Self-regulation involves your child's ability to take what she experiences and turn it into information she can use to control thoughts, emotions, and behaviors.

ACTIVITY

Theresa is sitting at the table with her parents, and they are all ready to eat. In their family they pass the food to one another, and the person waits to receive the dish in order to serve him- or herself. Mom serves herself some mashed potatoes and then passes the bowl to Theresa's brother, Hoyt. He then serves himself some mashed potatoes. Now the bowl reaches Theresa, and she takes her spoonful of food. Theresa says, "Thank you, Hoyt!"

INSIGHT

Theresa watches her mother and brother wait for the food to be handed to them so they can serve themselves. Theresa then takes these cues and uses her self-regulation skills to wait for her turn. She also spontaneously says thank you. This takes intentional effort on her part.

For instance, when your child stops playing and begins cleaning up when asked or impulsively shares a toy with a friend these are demonstrations that she has regulation of her emotions, thoughts, and behavior. **Much practice is required for your child to learn how to regulate herself in the first five years of her life.**

You play a key role in helping your child regulate her thinking and behavior. The best way to help her is through modeling during ordinary activities. Your child is getting cues from you, for instance, in situations that require turn taking, such as waiting to be served food.

Self-regulation is not a skill that stands alone; it also affects other areas such as cognitive development. **Thinking affects emotions, and emotions affect cognitive development.** When your child cannot self-regulate effectively, she will move from one activity to another as opposed to engaging in each one.

For instance, you have probably observed your child become frustrated during an activity and say, "I'm not good at this!" showing she cannot regulate her anxiety. She then walks away from the task, unable to persist in a challenging activity.

If your child uses self-regulation skills, she will say, "This is hard, but I can do it" (the emotion leads to positive self-esteem behavior). She will then try to figure out how to accomplish the task (the cognitive skill is persisting in problem solving).

Self-regulation requires your child to intentionally make a decision to do something other than what her impulsivity directs her to do. Think about a time when you witnessed your child take a friend's toy; you had to step in and help her return the toy. This resulted in her getting upset and crying. Your child was unable to use self-regulation skills and acted on the impulse of wanting the toy and taking it. As a parent, you know this behavior is not acceptable and involves thinking and emotions that do not support appropriate or effective social development.

Therefore, you must help your child develop self-regulation skills by using different strategies, such as modeling (playing a sharing game), using hints and cues ("Remember, whose crayon is that?"), and gradually withdrawing your support to let her practice these skills.

Modeling is how your child sees you react to situations. Cues are the directions and gestures you give to help her move in the right direction.

It is very similar to a mother bird and its baby: Mother bird shows her child how to fly and then she just has to let the baby do it herself. You show your child how to self-regulate, and then you have to let her try. You will have to demonstrate appropriate behavior more than once, and that is normal.

Helping your child learn to persist in difficult learning experiences is one of the most important results of developing her self-regulation skills. Also helping your child control her stress-based or anxious or angry emotions by modeling appropriate responses helps her develop into an emotionally well-balanced adult.

Self-Awareness >
Mirror, Mirror, on the Wall

Self-awareness refers to your child's ability to see himself as having a sense of belonging, being able to do things well, being independent, and being accepted.

As your child gains self-awareness he is beginning to answer the question, "Who am I?"

Your child sees his ability to successfully complete a given task. This develops as your child completes tasks and receives feedback about how he did. Self-awareness plays a role in the communication your child will have with others, and it is de-veloped by the experiences he has and the observations he makes.

An important part of under-standing your child's emotional development is the establishment of self-awareness, or your child's overall perception of self, including his own traits, habits, abilities, motives, and social roles.

Self-awareness supports self-

Self-awareness can best be explained by discussing the three steps it takes for your child to reach this state.

1. When your child was two years old he displayed **self-consciousness**, which is embarrassment or pride in situations such as looking at himself in a mirror.

2. Now at the age of three your child displays **self-awareness**. He knows that what he sees in the mirror is "I," not anyone else, staring back at him. He knows he has an identity.

3. The third step will occur between the ages of five and seven, when your child is able to see himself beyond the mirror experience. He can identify himself in a movie taken a few years back, or in a picture that shows him significantly younger and in different clothes. With your child understanding he has an identity, another aspect of self-awareness comes into the picture: **self-efficacy**, which is the belief that he can succeed in accomplishing what he puts his mind to.

identity. Self-identity supports your child in discovering "I." The discovery of "I" supports self-efficacy or "I can do it!" This all leads to confidence!

Self-efficacy creates positive emotions that your child needs to be successful in facing challenging tasks as he enters school.

Be sensitive and responsive as well as physically and emotionally available to your child. Promote trust, security, and exploration through nurturing relationships. Be consistent and create stimulating environments—all of these will support your child's development of self-awareness and positive self-esteem.

3. Language Development

> **Language encompasses all of the language arts: listening, speaking, reading, and writing. Language development is the way in which your child learns to communicate and understand spoken or written words.**

Three year olds use these skills now, creating a foundation for their use of language throughout their lives. A rich language environment is essential for the rapid development of a child's brain. Language and literacy are the links between learning to talk and learning to read.

When parents and caregivers speak with a child in a timely, responsive manner, the child learns new words and is soon able to hold a conversation. This can be a hard task to achieve sometimes, especially when you are doing several things at one time. For instance, let's say that your child has asked you, "Why do birds fly?" The question comes out of the blue, and it is not a topic you know much about. But it is a hot topic for your child! Take a moment, stop what you are doing, and say something like this, "Birds fly so that they can get from one place to another, like when we drive the car from the house to the store. It is their form of transportation." From this simple answer you have responded, introduced words like *transportation* and *drive*. You have also created a conversation opportunity for the two of you to talk back and forth.

Listening and Understanding

Emerging Literacy

Communication and Speaking

WHOLE CHILD: AGE THREE
Language
Development Components

Learning language and practicing communication skills help your child obtain information and express herself in a variety of ways and settings. These skills will help your child develop an expressive vocabulary, as well as learn to read and to communicate through writing. Your child is learning language by listening to others in her environment and by listening to a variety of books and simple stories. Through this process, your child will notice the sounds of language and may play with rhyming or finding other similar sounds.

Think about a simple rhyme like, "Rabbits." *"Rabbits-rabbits one, two, three, will you come and play with me? Camels-camels four, five, six, why do you have a hump like this?"* In just two lines your child has heard sounds of a rhyme, used counting skills, been pulled into a story about different animals, and been given an opportunity to interact by continuing the rhyming.

1. Listening and Understanding

Your child's communication involves much more than speech, and certainly more than writing, because her writing skills are still developing. She will communicate in many different ways by using nonverbal gestures, glances, and changes in tone of voice when speaking. How your child observes people in her environment helps develops her communication and speaking skills.

2. Communication and Speaking

Listening is an active process that has three steps:

1. *Hearing*—Your three year old listens just enough to catch what is being said.

2. *Understanding*—Your child takes what is heard and comprehends it.

3. *Judging*—After your child understands, she decides if it makes sense to her.

**3.
Emerging
Literacy**

Emerging literacy explains how your child uses knowledge of reading and writing skills before she actually learns how to read and write words. Three year olds are in the process of becoming literate. The process will continue through college and beyond.

Listening and Understanding >

New World, New Words

Listening and understanding involves your child paying attention to what someone says and making sense of what was heard.

Listening is a very important communication skill to teach your child; it is not a skill that develops naturally. Children this age especially have a great way of using selective listening skills, tuning out the things they do not want to hear.

ACTIVITY

Peter is playing a game of Simon Says with his parents. Peter loves this game. In a very slow voice his mom says, "Siiimon saaays touuuch your toessss." Peter listens then touches his toes. In a really fast voice Dad says, "Okay, touch your nose!" Peter touches his nose. "I didn't say Simon says, Peter. Listen for Simon says before you move." As his parents continue to take turns giving directions they each go faster and faster until no one can keep up.

INSIGHT

Peter has to listen and understand the question in order to produce the correct action. The instructions are simple yet fun enough to keep Peter entertained. Peter is also hearing vocabulary words *toes*, *nose*, and *touch*.

Your child's vocabulary expands as he understands what he hears and uses words he hears in his communication with others such as:

* **nouns**: *flower, banana, towel, bath;*

* **verbs**: action verbs (*walk, jump*), being verbs (I *am*, you *are*), helping verbs (Do you *need* a tissue?), and irregular verbs (The dog *bit* me, not, The dog bited me.);

* **adjectives**: *pretty, colorful, mad;*

* **adverbs**: *quickly, happily.*

These types of words are used more in your child's sentences because they signify a simplified manner of speech in which only the most important words are used to express ideas.

However, some children this age have cognitive limitations on the length of words they can produce. Given these limitations, they sensibly leave out the least important parts but still get their point across.

You might hear a your child say, "Adam make tower." As your child continues to expand his words, he will begin to use prepositions (*up, down, below*) and pronouns (*he, she, you*) along with the other words. He will now say, "*I* (pronoun) will *make* (verb) *my* (adjective) *tower* (noun) *on* (preposition) *grass* (noun)."

As you teach your child new words make them concrete by helping him visualize them. If it's an adjective like *scratchy*, point out the scratchiness on Dad's chin.

Your three year old's use of nouns, action verbs, and adjectives allows him to better understand the language he is using. Therefore, communicating with your three year old is one of the most important, pleasurable, and rewarding parts of your parenting experience. The more interactive conversations you have with your child, the more your child will learn to listen; the more you encourage the use of words, the more your child will understand.

Communication and Speaking >
Making More Sense

Your child will use a greater variety of closed-class words (e.g. prepositions) between now and four years of age.

Closed-class words or **function words** are limited in number and act as guides for sentence structure. The use of closed-class words makes your child's sentences easier to understand.

For example, as your child's language skills develop he will use the prepositions *in* and *on*. He will understand the preposition *under*. He will also use gestures to tell the meaning of locational prepositions (such as pointing).

Prepositions like on, in, under are easier for your child to understand than behind, beside, and between. Have you ever asked your child to bring you a ball? You give clues such as "It is in front of the door." Even with this clue, he still has difficulty locating the ball. This is because your child has to identify the relationship between the front and the back of an object (a ball has no identifiable parts). Therefore, for your child to use a preposition correctly, he must first understand its meaning. This skill develops beyond the age of three.

ACTIVITY

 Three-and-a-half year old Max points to some other children at the park and says to his dad, "They are eating ice cream on the grass and not making a big mess." If Max just said, "Eat ice cream no messy," it would have been more difficult for his dad to understand what he meant.

INSIGHT

 In order for Max to use the preposition (*on*) correctly and the adjective (*messy*) he has to expand his speech and word knowledge to communicate the meaning of what he is seeing. This comes with time and practice.

Phonology

Phonology is how speech/word sounds are used and organized in your child's language as he learns to talk. This area of development is a cognitive skill, and it is a strong predictor of future academic success. Your child was not born being able to make all the word choices and patterns of language.

He goes through this developmental process because he is learning to coordinate his tongue, lips, teeth, etc. Think back to the time when you heard your child say something such as "baba" for bottle. Even now, if your child just turned three, you may hear him say "nail" for "snail." As your child continues to develop, he will stop using incorrect speech sounds and articulate and enunciate increasingly complex sentences.

"They are eating ice cream on the grass and not making a big mess."

Emergent Literacy >
The Printed Word

Emergent or emerging literacy refers to how your child interacts with books; it also includes when she reads and writes, even if she cannot actually read or write in the traditional way.

The ways that your child will learn to read and write are similar to how she develops language.

Your child must learn about written language before she can read and write in the traditional way. Very early on your child becomes immersed in written language even if you do not do this intentionally by reading to her. This occurs as she sees environmental print—books, magazines, and advertisements on TV. Words are already a part of her world way before she can read or write them.

Did you know you instinctively engage in reading, writing, and talking experiences with your child on a daily basis? For example, every time you leave a note for your child in her lunch box for the teacher to read, share a story, label objects, communicate, or sign you are engaging in literacy. Interactions between you and your child cannot occur all the time; it is for this reason your child has already started thinking about written language.

Just as your child wants to learn written language, she also becomes excited about using pictures and letters to communicate. She will use symbols invented by herself as printed words; this may include poorly copied words, gestures, or marks on paper.

Reading starts for your child when she gives meaning to the symbols around her, such as stop signs, labels on food, symbols on an electronic device or a restaurant billboard. Take a moment to look at your child's "writing." She will write lots of wavy lines; interspersed between the wavy lines you will see a symbol that looks like a circle or another kind of shape.

If you were to ask her what she "wrote," she may say, "I wrote your name and mine." This is how your child is showing emerging literacy skills with her attempt at writing, using symbols to represent print.

Through natural exposure to books and print and through conversations with people, your child will discover that written words are another way to communicate. Three year olds continue to grow in understanding and in their use of language.

As her vocabulary continues to grow, your child will be able to produce longer and more complex sentences. During the preschool period, children's speech becomes clearer as they master new sounds and new syllable structures.

Learning to read and write must be a gradual process that is nurtured over time. Parents should be intentional in providing activities to support development of these skills. Activities include parents having purposeful conversations with their children and children having purposeful conversations with other children; this will support language development.

Provide your child with access to many different books and other reading and writing materials. It is important to also offer opportunities for exploring and engaging in literacy activities, which include reading, writing, and learning letters and sounds.

Your child's learning in literacy cannot be separated from her learning in other areas (e.g. fine motor skills). Her interest in various subjects and activities can fuel her verbal language and create opportunities for learning to read and write.

For instance, you might have recently taken a family vacation; on the trip, your child sees dolphins and whales. This experience can result in looking at pictures of different types of whales, naming those pictures, seeing the names in print, and making up stories about the whales. This is teaching and supporting literacy in a natural way based on your child's current interests and environment. The more you read and speak and engage with your child, the more her emerging literacy will lead to actual literacy—reading and writing on her own.

Storytelling

Storytelling is developed from social interactions and play scenarios that children have with each other and adults.

It is amazing to see how three year olds have learned the art of story-telling: how to sequence events, how to set actions in place and time, and how to organize a story around characters. It is hard to imagine that this is possible when they are still in the midst of developing elementary language skills.

Another way in which children acquire storytelling skills is through talking about the past with their parents. A child might say, "Mommy, do you remember when we went to the ice cream store?" This starts the story, and the adult and child will then build on the story together.

Children tend to talk about experiences they have with others; this builds intimacy between parents and children. Storytelling is a three-phase process in your child's development; it begins even before she turns three. In the beginning of storytelling, your child will listen to stories that you tell. She will watch your face, listen to your voice, and take cues from you on how the story should end.

ACTIVITY

Wini is playing with a doll. She holds the doll in her arms as she gives it a drink. Wini says, "Let's have milk! There you go, dolly, are you happy? You drank your milk. Do you want more? You burped! Mommy can get you more milk. Here you go. Drink it slow."

INSIGHT

Wini has just told a story through her play. It has a beginning (having milk), middle (drank all of the milk), and an end (more milk). She even includes characters (dolly) and emotions (happy).

Next, when your child has learned all she can from you about telling stories, you will hear your child add elements to the story you started that you never imagined. By the time your child has turned three, you have a certified storyteller who captivates the attention of all who will listen.

Organizing Stories

Your child can organize stories when she is able to give descriptions of the setting (faraway place), give detailed information about the characters (he was so big), and provide a sequence of action to communicate a story verbally.

Young children follow different strategies when organizing their stories. One of these is called **centering**.

With centering, your child will create a story around a central topic. Each object, action, or event included in the story relates to the topic, but the listener may have difficulty recognizing the relationship between them. Your child will give you as much lively detail as she can about the story. You may hear your child say, "A Mars bar bush growing out of the earth." Remember: You will have difficulty understanding; that is normal.

ACTIVITY

 The following story told by three-year-old Eve to her friend Nathan about her day at the park with a pink burger (topic) provides an example of centering. "I ate a pink burger like this," mimes eating, "with the swings" (detail), "I was high" (detail). "Mommy threw the ball" (detail), "burger" (topic), "like this. I didn't get the burger ball. My burger is pink. I liked my pink burger. I had chips with my burger, chips pink just like my burger."

INSIGHT

This is a perfect example of Eve having a topic and using detail in her story. It is very difficult for the adult listener to put all the pieces together. For two three year olds the story makes sense. Eve demonstrates her early ability to organize her story for the listener. Remember, organizing has a setting (park), characters (pink burger and Mommy), and a sequence of actions (swinging, throwing a ball, and eating chips).

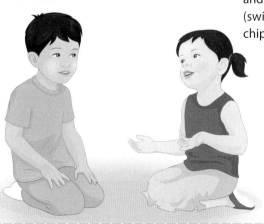

"I had chips with my burger, chips pink just like my burger."

4. Creative Development

> **Creative development activities invite your child to listen, observe, move, solve problems, and imagine while using several operating systems.**

Creative development consists of your child's participation in art, music, movement and dance, and dramatic play. Active involvement in creative arts promotes learning and brain development. Three years of age is a good time for parents to continue to support their children's imaginative thinking and self-expression and enhance their growth in these areas.

Children can count musical beats, experiment with colors to make a new one, create a dialogue for a story, or move like animal characters in a book. Activities like these will support development in the social, cognitive, and creative processes. Creative play activates the mind and senses, allowing children to expand or contract their universe and shape it any way they please with whichever characters, objects, words, or music they choose.

WHOLE CHILD: AGE THREE
Creative
Development Components

1. Music

Music involves listening to, learning about, and making melody or harmony. Your child will listen and respond to different kinds of music by moving her body, dancing, painting, or talking about how the music is making her feel. Music can include all types of instruments, songs, singing, and live or recorded music.

2. Dance

Dance includes movement and moving the body in different ways, which enables her to learn what her body can do and how to express herself. Your child will imitate how animals move or how to move when happy or sad.

3. Visual Arts

Visual art involves giving three year olds the opportunity to explore materials through painting, drawing, mixing colors, making 3-D sculptures, and creating mosaic patterns. Participating in visual art enables children to explore their environment and discover connections and meanings using art materials to express and communicate their discoveries.

4. Dramatic Play

Dramatic play is when your child pretends to be a "teacher," for example, and gives a lesson to a younger child. It includes your child pretending and mimicking what she sees, as well as her having the opportunity to take an object and use it for anything she can imagine.

Have various instruments available to your child to encourage her to experiment with melody, rhythm, and sound to create music on her own.

Remember, the Whole Child Parenting Program offers appropriate developmental products and monthly activity books that walk you through supporting your child's skills. Using these in conjunction with the recommended age-appropriate room materials ensures faster development.

Music >
Rhythm in My Bones

Music is a vocal or instrumental sound that is combined or done separately to create a melody, harmony, or rhythm.

ACTIVITY

Michael is in his bedroom looking outside through the window. It's raining. He puts on his headphones, closes his eyes, and starts singing "Itsy Bitsy Spider." He sings it again, this time doing the actions with his hands.

The itsy bitsy spider
climbed up the waterspout.
Down came the rain
and washed the spider out.
Out came the sun
and dried up all the rain.
And the itsy bitsy spider
climbed up the spout again.

INSIGHT

This is a song Michael has sung in music class with his friends. By doing the actions and singing the song he demonstrates his ability to listen and understand. Singing reinforces the rhyme staying in his memory. This is how literacy and music come together. His ability to sing and chant will help develop language skills and auditory discrimination.

Your child enjoys listening to all musical styles.

Just hearing a specific type of music over and over does not seem to affect your child's listening preferences, but your approval and support do have a positive influence on your child's musical preferences. By nature, music is a social experience because it is shared with others as your child shows you how he sings, dances, or plays instruments.

Music is also an area of creative development that provides your child opportunities to enhance his cognitive thinking skills by providing practice in patterns, math concepts, and symbolic thinking skills.

As your child learns to distinguish different sounds in music, his thinking and memory skills will grow. Repeating songs he has heard before helps your child remember sounds and words in order for a certain amount of time.

These skills are learned through the enjoyment of music. For instance, many children's songs have counting in them, such as "One, Two, Buckle My Shoe" or "Five Little Monkeys." The rhythms of these songs make it easier for your child to absorb math concepts.

Singing is natural for your child. Parents frequently hear their child break into a song or chanting; these chants are not true songs but consist of repeated tones. Physical, rhythmic movement, such as walking, hopping, pounding, or rocking, may accompany singing and chanting (e.g. "Ants Go Marching").

Don't get too ahead of your child's development at age three. Even though he breaks into spontaneous chants, he is still having difficulty carrying a tune.

Dance >
Moving and Grooving

Dance is defined as creativity through movement; this involves your child's problem solving, self-expression, and imagination skills.

The random movements of the infant and the spontaneous swaying and bouncing to music of the toddler develop into the more dance-like movements of your three year old.

He is motivated to dance to music, but his movements are not always coordinated to the music he hears. Thus a steady beat, rhythm, or overall musical effect may still not be accurately connected to his body movements, though he is moving closer to coordinating himself to the music. Simple exercises in movement are best to encourage skill development for this age child.

Your child loves having a dance partner. Set a time during the day to dance with your child to different genres of music.

As you encourage dancing in your child, you also encourage him to express himself and be creative. This will help him later in life as he learns to improve his coordination, build his spatial awareness skills, and think through ways of how to move his body.

ACTIVITY

Tito and his friend are in music class. The teacher says, "How about if we sing my favorite song about dancing trees?" She stands up. "How tall are trees? Children, stand up and grab a friend's hand as you dance and sway like me."

She begins to sing, "He swings and he sways and he shakes all his limbs. The little ole tree loves to dance with the wind. He rustles and bustles when the wind comes to call. He dances so hard I'm afraid he will fall." Tito and his friend love the song so much because they are swaying and dancing to the beat. They also get to tumble to the floor at the end. The boys want the teacher to sing the song again.

INSIGHT

This class is a great example of helping children use problem-solving skills as each one thinks about which direction to sway, shake, swing, and dance. This simple activity fosters development of both imagination—each child has to first imagine dancing like a tree—and self-expression.

Your child can move fast or slowly and stop and turn with some smoothness and control, but he still has difficulty understanding that a relationship exists between the sounds he hears and what his muscles can do. Thus, your child will limit his movements, repeating a few patterns consistently during his musical experience. To unlock creativity, think along the lines of facilitating music and movement with him. Present a challenge or question to which there are many possible ways your child can move his body in response (e.g. Can you move your legs?).

A dance session will require mental concentration and active participation from your child. **Dance will help your child become aware of his own body and learn gross motor coordination skills. These are critical to other developmental skills.**

Dance gives your child a sense of accomplishment in his abilities as he learns new steps and ways to move his body and work together with his dance partner—that's you! Dancing together provides a fun and physically beneficial bonding experience.

Visual Arts >
Artist

Visual art is anything your child produces that can be seen. This can be a drawing, a painting, a photo she takes of an object, or a sculpture she makes from clay.

ACTIVITY

 Mom is sitting in the kitchen with Dad while Taylor is taking her afternoon nap. Mom says, "I saw Taylor drawing today. I wanted to draw with her." Dad asks, "Why didn't you?" Mom replies, "I can't draw very well, and I really didn't want Taylor to see what I was doing so I just sat and watched her."

INSIGHT

In this situation Mom's lack of drawing skills and lack of creative confidence causes her to worry about transferring her deficits to Taylor. Rather than doing this, Mom should show her confidence in herself and sit down to draw beside her daughter. It is important to engage in art with your child and enjoy the process, not worry about the end product.

Art builds self-confidence in your child because your child believes that she can draw, and she enjoys drawing. **The amazing thing with children is that they have no fear of engaging in artistic activities especially when you build their confidence.**

Engage in the following to support your child's art experiences at home:

* Do you help your child feel good about her art? By saying something like this, "I love how you used the color blue in your picture. It reminds me of the ocean." Don't name objects in the painting for your child because your meaning could differ from your child's; let her tell you what something is.

* Do you engage in art with your child? Sit at the kitchen table and do a coloring page with her.

* Do you give your child different ways to use art materials? Give your child crayons and let her make crayon shavings using an automatic pencil sharpener. Then glue those shavings to a piece of construction paper. Then cut it into stars or other shapes. Add string and you have a mobile!

* Do you have a special place to display your child's artwork? Make space on the kitchen refrigerator or kitchen walls and use letter magnets to hold up the art.

> *** Art promotes creativity.**
> *** Creativity brings out your child's personality and builds her self-esteem.**

Encourage your child to experiment with art products in the following ways:

* Have faith in your child's artwork and tell her you like her art.
* Refrain from offering too much help.
* Accept your child's creative products without placing a value judgment on them.
* State the confidence you have in your child to make the project her own.

When you view your child's artwork and ask questions, she realizes the creative process involved is of great value to you. In other words, the process is more important than the product you want to hang on your wall or refrigerator. To allow for true creativity there must be no boundaries to what she is allowed to make or draw.

Dramatic Play >
Playing House!

Dramatic play is
when your child
transforms into
something he is not;
it fuels imagination
and is driven by the
materials available
to him as well as the
experiences he has
had.

*If you just went for a checkup
you might see your child take
on the role of doctor. He may
become an astronaut and turn
the house into a spaceship after
watching a movie about aliens.*

During dramatic play, you will see your child take on a new role—and he would love for you to join in. Your child will use many different areas of the house as settings for dramatic play.

You should offer many opportunities for your child to engage in role-playing and make-believe activities by having a play area in your home with seating and storage for a wide variety of props, such as boards, scrap lumber, dress-up clothes, cooking utensils, banners, signs, and other items that support dramatic play. You don't have to go out and buy these things; simply look for unused items around your house or ask a neighbor.

Dramatic play offers opportunities for your child to use and expand his creative life skills and mimic what he sees you do. These activities will help him make meaning of his environment.

Even without any props, your child will engage in dramatic play by telling stories and acting them out. Imagine how much fun you could have participating in this important developmental skill together. Take a chance. Play a part. You're missing out if you don't give it a shot!

Here are some steps you can take to support dramatic play:

1. Focus on the process of dramatic play by asking questions that help to extend the experience. Your son is making honking noises as he pushes a race car on the carpet. Mom: "Where is that race car going?" or "That is a fast car. What is it honking at?"

2. Model your own creative thinking and expression by making up voices and sound effects. Using recycled items for a microphone (e.g. a can of soda).

3. When your little one says he wants to role play a character, encourage the problem-solving process by asking open-ended questions such as "What will you need to be the character?" Questions like these help your three year old recognize the creative process in himself.

5. Physical Development

> By the beginning of her third year, your child is becoming very active and agile.

You see your child spend a lot of time getting to know her body and how to control it. In accordance with how three year olds develop, parents will see that their children will gain about four to five pounds, grow at a rate of two to three inches, and reach about half of their adult height during the third year. Because of these advancements, your child will discover just how much her fine motor and gross motor skills have improved.

Your child's balancing abilities increase in the way that she walks, runs, and jumps. Your child jumps on two feet, and she can catch a smaller ball than she could at age two. Your three year old is super excited because now she can pedal a tricycle, which will prepare her for a bicycle. Your child can hop on one foot, copy a circle, and place small objects in a small opening. Because she loves to move and be active, it is a perfect time to support further growth in physical development. As we learn more about gross motor (large muscle) and fine motor (small muscle) development, you will be given support and solutions to help your child advance her physical skills.

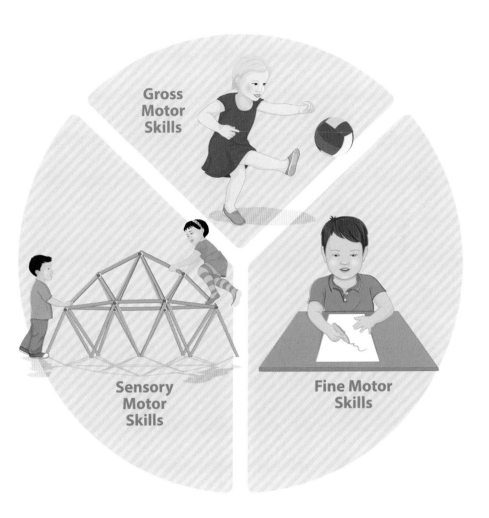

WHOLE CHILD: AGE THREE
Physical
Development Components

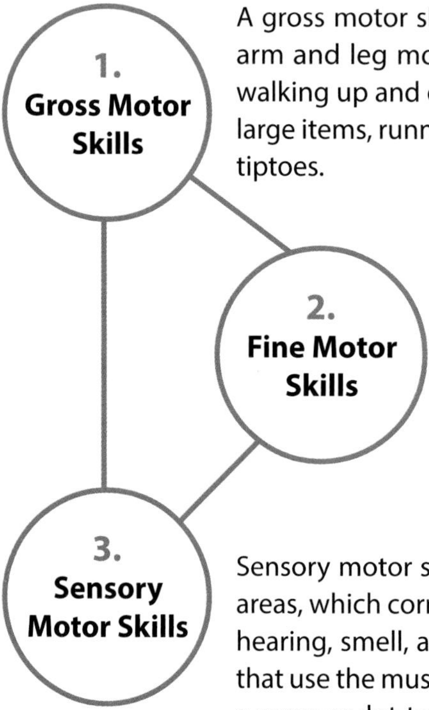

1. Gross Motor Skills

A gross motor skill is your child's ability to control arm and leg movements. This includes climbing, walking up and down stairs, kicking a ball, carrying large items, running short distances, or standing on tiptoes.

2. Fine Motor Skills

Fine motor development applies to small movements of the hands, wrists, fingers, feet, and toes. Fine motor skills also include smaller actions, such as grasping an object between the thumb and a finger or using the lips and the tongue to taste an object.

3. Sensory Motor Skills

Sensory motor skills in three year olds include five areas, which correspond to the senses: touch, sight, hearing, smell, and taste. Touch can involve games that use the muscles; sight can be used to complete a maze or dot-to-dot puzzle; hearing might include playing listening games; smell can be experimenting with plants and flowers in the garden; and taste might involve trying different kinds of foods.

The ability to kick a ball indicates a big jump in gross motor skill development.

Remember, the Whole Child Parenting Program offers appropriate developmental products and monthly activity books that walk you through supporting your child's skills. Using these in conjunction with the recommended age-appropriate room materials ensures faster development.

Gross Motor Skills >

Developing the Large Muscles

Gross motor skills are skills that involve moving different body parts such as feet, legs, head, and arms.

Gross motor skills are important because they are the foundation for your child having the ability to do more complex skills, like karate or little kid soccer.

Gross motor skills can be broken down into three areas: loco-motor skills, balance skills, and ball skills. All of these gross motor skills are necessary for your child to move through life with confidence as he learns to play games and sports and engage in other, more complex activities like swimming.

Your child needs a lot of opportunities for physical development in these specific areas; therefore, active play is important for getting those large muscles moving. Gross motor skills develop through activities in which your child has the opportunity to move his legs, arms, and lower body.

1. Loco-motor skills—Running, jumping, hopping, and leaping forward are examples. Mickey stands with his knees bent and his arms stretched in back of him; he then propels himself forward and leaps, landing on his feet.

2. Balance skills—are movements in which your child's body remains in place, but moves in a horizontal or vertical direction. With his arms bent and lifted to waist level during take off, Nicholas steps forward with his lead foot followed by a step from the foot behind as he gallops forward.

3. Ball skills—are throwing, kicking, and catching. Mark prepares to catch the ball by holding both hands in front of his body with his elbows slightly bent. He stretches his arms in front of himself to reach the ball as it comes to him.

ACTIVITY

Mom decides that her son needs something to do since it is raining outside. She finds masking tape in the drawer and tapes down a straight line on the floor. Mom asks her son to walk on the tape with his arms stretched out and try not to fall to the right or left of the tape.

INSIGHT

Mom supports her son's physical development when she encourages him to use his legs and arms to balance.

Help your child develop new skills:

1. **Observe the behavior in others**, e.g. Tommy watches Dad shoot a basketball through the hoop.

2. **Form a mental image of the behavior**, e.g. Tommy then visualizes how his dad bends his knees and propels the ball up with his arms.

3. **Imitate the behavior**, e.g. Tommy then stands next to Dad, bends his knees, and propels the ball up with his arms.

4. **Practice the behavior**, e.g. Tommy does not get the ball through the hoop the first time, so he tries again.

5. **Be motivated to repeat the behavior**, e.g. Tommy's dad says, "You can do it," which motivates Tommy to keep trying.

Three year olds need a lot of opportunities for physical development; active play is important for getting those large muscles moving.

When your child is having difficulty kicking a ball, first give him a moment to try to solve the problem on his own. Then you can help your child problem solve using a different strategy that you illustrate for him so he can learn to kick the ball better. Then help your child think about how he could practice this new skill.

Fine Motor Skills >
Developing the Small Muscles

Fine motor skills refer to
the movements we make
with the small muscles of
the hands, wrist, and
fingers.

Children start to use their hands right at birth to explore their own bodies and the world around them. Their fine motor skills develop as their bodies start to move more in different ways and become more stable in their movements.

During his third year child will be able to hold a crayon or pencil in his fingers instead of his fist, draw or color a picture, and copy simple lines. He will be able to cut paper with scissors, although not in a straight line; manipulate small objects; put together simple puzzles; and stack blocks. He will be able to turn the page of a book and begin to lace—but not tie—his shoes.

The two popular terms that come up when learning about fine motor skills in three year olds are **fist grip** and **pincer grip**. An example of a fist grip is when your child uses his whole hand and wraps it around a pencil to write his name. A pincer grip refers to the pinching muscles that use the thumb and pointer finger.

ACTIVITY

 Andy is at home with his dad playing in his dad's office. He asks his dad for a pencil and some paper so that he can "write" his mommy a letter. He takes the pencil and looks at his dad, and then he tries to hold the pencil like his dad, but ends up making a fist. Dad stops what he is doing and shows Andy how to hold the pencil with his thumb and pointer finger.

INSIGHT

As Andy learns to fine-tune his pincer grip he still has a tendency to hold his pencil with a fist. Even though many children do the same thing until they are five, it is really okay only for a toddler to do this. Andy should have mastered this skill already, so his father should keep practicing with him to help him nail it down.

Even if your child has not mastered a fine motor skill it is never too late to teach him. Take the time to stop what you're doing and show your child how to develop his skills.

Your child can get lots of practice with fine motor skills by engaging in simple activities such as zipping and unzipping zippers, picking up connecting blocks or finger foods, and stringing beads. Strengthening the pincer grasp is an important skill because it will prepare your child for holding pencils, markers, crayons, and paintbrushes, which support the development of prewriting skills.

Wrist control and finger strength are also important parts of ultimately mastering writing and drawing. Fitting pieces into a puzzle will develop dexterity of the hand and wrist.

All types of fine motor skills are important to practice. Practicing and mastering one fine motor skill can lead to the development or refinement of another. Practice is key.

Sensory Motor Skills >

The Five Senses

Sensory motor skills involve the ability to use fine motor skills or gross motor skills through the senses of touch, smell, taste, sight, and hearing.

As your three year old spends more time moving, listening, touching, and smelling, he will learn more through the opportunities you provide to interact with his surroundings while using his senses. Try some of the activities on the next page.

ACTIVITY

Hollis and Anne are restless. They've been inside doing art and playing with blocks for hours and need to get moving. The children ask permission to go out and play. Their mom is more than happy to encourage outdoor play, and she opens the door with enthusiasm. The kids run outside, straight for the climbing structure happy to be free of the four walls of their home.

INSIGHT

Your child must use fine motor skills to coordinate eye and hand movements and to adjust his grip on playground equipment. He must coordinate the action of climbing and using many large muscle groups to maintain his balance.

Do the following activities with your child to encourage sensory development:

* Squirt a small amount of shaving cream onto the kitchen table. Ask your child how it smells, then ask if he has ever seen someone in the house use shaving cream (getting him to think and pull from his memory to develop his cognitive skills). Encourage your child to draw shapes or animals in the shaving cream, making a game out of the experience.

* Mimic Me is the name of this step in the game. Write the first letter of your child's name on a piece of white paper. Use a black marker and write in very large print. Ask your child to mimic you and draw the letter they see on the paper.

This type of activity helps your child in the following ways: Your child must pay attention to the letter you wrote on the paper; he must focus to draw the same letter in the shaving cream; he must use his fine motor skills to hold out only his pointer finger to draw the letter; and he must use his hand-eye coordination skills to get it all on target. Sight, touch, and smell are involved in the activity above.

Even though larger muscles usually develop before smaller muscles, more advanced motor abilities require your child to coordinate large motor (large muscle) skills with small motor (small muscle) skills.

6. Health and Care

> **All children grow at different rates. Your child's growth rate will include genetic and environmental factors.**

Environment plays a role in your child's growth because the conditions of your child's environment are important in how she progresses both physically and emotionally. It is crucial for parents to understand the different aspects of environment to ensure that their children are getting what they need to grow and develop. One aspect in their environment is **nurture**: the loving, responsive care you give that has an effect on how your child grows. When your child feels loved and supported, she can focus on learning and growing instead of worrying. **Nutrition** is another environmental factor. Good nutrition leads to growth; offering a variety of foods to your child will give her the nutrients and vitamins needed for her brain and body to grow.

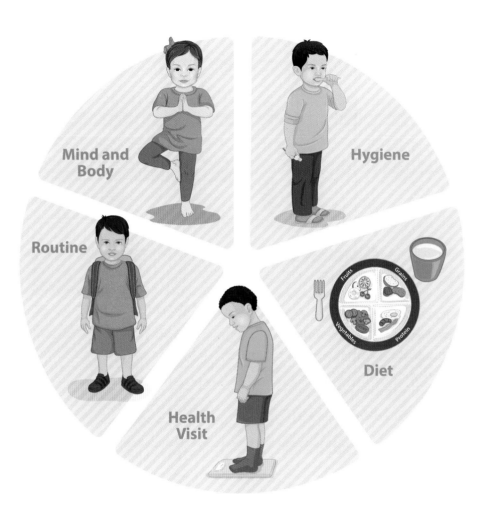

WHOLE CHILD: AGE THREE

Health and Care

Hygiene >
Keeping Clean, Oral Care, First Aid

I'm Clean!

Good health is connected to grooming and hygiene. It is important for your child to learn the importance of personal hygiene to avoid the spread of illness. **At three years of age, it is necessary for parents to guide and tell their children about personal hygiene and set the example.** Good hygiene skills will help your child the rest of her life.

Teaching hygiene may seem difficult and frustrating at times as your child may boycott taking a bath, brushing her teeth for two minutes, or even washing and combing her hair. You can read books to your child as a means of keeping hygiene practices in her mind. Elizabeth Verdick has an entire series of books for children ranging from *Germs Are Not for Sharing* to *Noses Are Not for Picking*.

Don't forget washing clothes; now that your child is three, she can help you sort the laundry by color and even drop clothes into the machine. Remember, you are the role model; what she sees you do will set your child on the path to healthy hygiene practices in the future.

Because your three year old has better listening and understanding skills, she can understand why she needs to:

* bathe regularly,
* brush her teeth twice a day,
* use tissues to blow her nose,
* cough into the crook of her arm,
* comb and brush her hair,
* and change her clothes daily.

Your child is capable of understanding not only the reasons for good hygiene, but also what happens when you don't practice good hygiene.

Oral Care

The American Academy of Pediatrics and the American Academy of Pediatric Dentistry recommend that you take your child to the dentist within six months after her first tooth erupts, or by her first birthday, whichever comes first.

After your child's first visit, the dentist will tell you when your child needs to return. Most children see a dentist every six months.

Just as you took the time to prepare your child for his well-child visit you need to do the same for a dental visit.

When your child was a toddler, you may have noticed that she had an inclination to want to brush her teeth herself; however, your child still needs your assistance when brushing. **Young children do not have the ability to brush their teeth effectively.**

To help your child still have a sense of independence, you can let her brush her teeth using a pea size amount of toothpaste, but then you must brush her teeth again to make sure no spots are missed.

The general rule is when your child is able to tie her own shoes, she can brush her own teeth because you will know her fine motor skills are developed enough to do this; however, you still need to monitor your child and make sure she is brushing for a full two minutes.

Correct brushing techniques

You can have your child lie down on a bed with her head in your lap, or you can have your child sit with her body between your legs and her head tilted back into your arms. You can also do this standing in front of the sink with your child's head tilted back.

Brush the teeth gently using small, circular motions, being sure to include the area where the teeth meet the gums. Start by brushing the outside surface and then move into the inside, brushing the bottom of the teeth last. Remember to use a circular motion. As you assist your child, use a timer so that she can help you track the two minutes.

First Aid

Your child will get bumps and bruises, cuts and sores. It is difficult for a parent to see a child get hurt. It is our natural instinct to protect our children from all injuries, and when we can't we feel we have somehow failed in our responsibilities.

It is very important to attend to your child's emotional needs while doing a quick assessment of the injury, moving close to her body and listening for a regular heart beat and breathing to insure these functions have not been compromised. When you have determined no other medical attention is needed outside of ice, a bandage, and/or washing, give your little one a hug, a kiss, and some cuddle time, letting your child know you care and are there to help.

Every parent needs a well-stocked first-aid kit at home and in the car for on the go. Kits for the house and car should be big enough to hold a wide range of supplies.

It is important to have the necessary first-aid materials for patching up a wound and calming your little one so you can make the boo-boo better.

Burns

1. Place under cold water.
2. If there is no broken skin, apply a burn cream, not petroleum jelly.
3. If there is broken skin, apply antibiotic ointment and a bandage.

Call a doctor as soon as possible if burns are on the face, hands, or if they are larger than ¼ inch anywhere on the body.

Splinters

1. Clean the area of the splinter with soap and water.
2. If the splinter is small and does not hurt, it will make its way out in a few days.
3. If the splinter is big, clean a pair of tweezers with alcohol and pull the splinter out. If the tip of the splinter breaks, you can sometimes nudge out a splinter with the edge of a credit card.
4. Wash the skin again.
5. If the splinter isn't out after a few days or is causing your child pain, turning red, or has pus, see your doctor to have it safely removed.

Bumps and Bruises

1. Place ice on the bumps.
2. Apply over-the-counter ointments for bruising or muscle aches.
3. Have your child rest.

Cuts and Scrapes

1. Wash your own hands.
2. Wash the cut with soap and water.
3. Pat dry.
4. Bandage the cut or scrape to keep out dirt and germs.

If the skin is broken, apply a thin layer of an over-the-counter antibiotic ointment, then cover with a bandage or gauze and surgical tape.

Apply pressure to the wound if it is still bleeding. If bleeding does not stop after 10 minutes, head to the emergency room because your child may need stitches. Head to the doctor also if your child's cut is longer than half an inch, there is something stuck inside the cut, or the cut is on your child's face because it may leave a noticeable scar if untreated.

* Antibacterial lotion (not petroleum jelly) can help clean the cut and should be applied with each bandage change; however, avoid rubbing alcohol and hydrogen peroxide because they can cause discomfort for your child and slow the healing process.

* Make sure to clean the cut, use an antibiotic cream or ointment, and keep it under a protective bandage. Change the bandage daily. After a few days, remove the bandage and allow the cut to air dry. This will lead to the formation of a scab, which shows the wound is healing. Encourage your child to leave the scab in place as it will fall off naturally and lessen the chance of scarring.

Diet >

Three year olds need:

* grains: 4–5 ounces (half from whole sources),
* vegetables: 1 ½ cups,
* fruits: 1–1 ½ cups,
* milk: 2 cups,
* meat and beans: 3–4 ounces.

When it comes to your child's diet it is your responsibility to set an example by making sure your child has healthful food options at every meal.

Active three year olds need between 1,200 and 1,600 calories each day. Compared to a toddler, a three year old has a smaller stomach and energy needs relative to her size, so she tends to stay full on a smaller amount of food.

It is important at this age to be cautious of portion sizes and how much your child eats. It is especially important to make sure you give small portions of any treats or high-fat foods because these can cause her to want to overeat.

We want to give our three year olds the best nutrition, but knowing how to do that without giving in to quick fixes of empty calories can be challenging.

Foods to Introduce at Three

Around the age of three, it's time to switch to skim or 1% milk and find more healthy fats and oils for your child in sources such as nuts and full-fat cheeses. Limit the amount of milk and juice your child drinks, especially between meals, because it can make your child not hungry for solids.

It is important to keep up with a routine of regularly planned snacks and meals so that your child can eat throughout the day. This helps her not overeat and be able to recognize her own hunger cues.

High-Fiber Foods

As your child grows older, the recommended portion will increase to roughly 14 grams of fiber per 1,000-calorie intake.

Fruits and vegetables are excellent sources of fiber, so you should encourage your child to eat as many as possible. Other high-fiber foods include beans, whole grain breads, and cereals.

> **To figure out how much fiber your child (age 3–18) needs, take the child's age and add 5. The sum is the number of grams of fiber your child should have each day.**
> **For example, for a 3-year-old child:**
> **3 + 5 = 8 grams of fiber.**

Other high-fiber foods that are over 5 grams of fiber include barley, navy beans, baked beans, split peas, lentils, wheat flour, refried beans, prunes, and spinach, just to name a few. Many of these foods may be new to your three year old, so show them to your child before you cook them and let her learn a little about them. We want to help that picky eater consume more high-fiber foods.

A high fiber diet should be used to:

* relieve and/or prevent constipation,
* increase stool volume,
* help manage the symptoms of irritable bowel syndrome.

Family Style Eating

Your three year old's diet should now reflect your family's diet in the types of foods she is eating. Now is a good time to start introducing manners at the dinner table.

Try to have all meals at a table. This will help your child establish more routine meal times.

It is also a great time to socialize and have family time with your child. Practice those language skills with your child and model the back and forth of conversation.

Lastly, you can model manners and safe eating habits. Put food in bowls and encourage your child to serve herself with a spoon. Have your child say *please* and *thank you* when she wants more of something, use a napkin, and help her clean up any spills.

Finding time to eat with your family may actually leave you feeling less stressed. Plan ahead by preparing the protein part of your meals for the week on a Sunday. Leave salad, vegetables, and fruit for right before. Planning cuts down on prep time.

Health Visit >
Healthy and On Track

Height and Weight

One of the most important ways your pediatrician will determine your child's physical growth is by measuring height and weight to make sure she is growing at a steady rate. Most three year olds fall between these two numbers (but don't worry, all children grow at different rates): Three-year-old girls range from 35 to 40 inches in height, and boys are roughly a half inch taller. Girls typically weigh 25 to 38 pounds, and boys weigh 27 to 38 pounds. In order to determine how your child compares to other children your doctor will use the pediatric growth chart.

As long as your child is growing at a regular rate, the position she holds on the chart is not terribly important.

Keep a monthly log of your child's height and weight to see how your three year old is growing.

Another measurement your doctor will take is the circumference of your child's head. This is important for determining healthy brain development.

Head Circumference:

Girls: 18.25 to 20 inches
Boys: 18.5 to 20.5 inches

Questions doctors may ask:

* Is your child still taking an afternoon nap? (Most still need one.)

* How much and how often does your child eat? Is he eating a variety of foods?

* How is potty training going? If your child hasn't shown any signs of being ready to toilet train, be sure to let your doctor know.

* Is he left- or right-handed? By age three, most children have a dominant hand.

* Does your child play well with others? Three year olds normally have a hard time sharing their toys.

* Can your child recognize his name when called out or in print?

* Does your child jump, kick a ball, or ride a tricycle or other three-wheeled bicycle?

* Does your child always wear a safety helmet while riding a bike or a scooter and while roller skating or inline skating?

Other important areas your doctor will discuss with you is how your child is progressing in his self-help skills, language skills, social skills, and behavioral development by asking the following questions:

* Does your child dress and undress himself (with a little help)?

* Does your child brush his teeth, wash hands, and brush his hair?

* Is your child able to form sentences using three or more words?

* Does your child walk up stairs with alternating feet?

Having routine yearly well-child visits with your little one's pediatrician enables you to address concerns (if any) early on, and give you peace of mind in knowing that your child is healthy and that his development is on track and age appropriate.

Routine >
Every Day the Same, Sleeping, Starting Preschool, and Safety

Every Day the Same

Routines and consistency are very important when it comes to your child's development and overall happiness. Your child will also begin to have expectations and pick up on cues when it comes to discipline, sleeping, and eating habits.

Your child has a hard time understanding why one day you read her a story before bed and another day you are too busy. Being consistent and reading a short bedtime story every night can help your child know that after the story she will be left in her room to sleep. That can be more comforting than just putting her in bed at a different time with a different routine every day.

Tattling occurs a lot at age three. In most cases, it is not because your child is trying to get another child in trouble. **Children at this age tattle when they see another child doing something they were told not to do; they are testing you to see if the rule set earlier still stands.**

In addition to handling tattling, try not to overreact when your child starts to tell stories or lies. Your child's imagination is growing, so she may just be testing out a story to see your reaction. She may lie about something she did, such as denying she broke a toy. Your response can be "We can fix this together" or "I understand that you don't feel good about breaking the toy."

It is also important to be consistent with discipline.

Your discipline must be clear, consistent, and immediate so that your child makes the connection between her act and the disciplinary action you take. Disciplinary actions should also make sense whenever possible. If she took something without asking, limit her time with that thing. If she broke something on purpose, have her make amends to the owner. Also note if your child is hungry or tired as these two states often lead to misbehavior.

Sleeping

Three year olds should start becoming pretty consistent with their sleeping. Most three year olds still take a nap during the day and generally sleep a total of 11 to 12 hours a day overall.

Try not to overschedule your child with activities, and respect her naptime. Do not sign up your child for a soccer class that starts at the same time your child naps. She will be cranky and won't enjoy being there because she is tired. Also, it is important to be active, but having too many activities going on every day can be exhausting. Make sure your child has some time every day to choose what she wants to do.

Talk to your doctor if your child is having trouble sleeping or wakes up constantly in the middle of the night. Nightmares are common at three years old because your preschooler's imagination is very active.

Nightmares can be inescapable, but having a daily routine and consistent naptime can alleviate any extra stress or irritability when going to sleep, which can trigger nightmares.

If your child has a nightmare, it is important to comfort her and help your child fall back asleep, especially between the ages of two and six.

Your three year old is maturing more and more each day, and now is the time to help her get a good night's sleep by doing the following:

1. Move your child to a big bed and out of the toddler bed. Give a lot of praise when she sleeps in it.

2. If your child gets up because she is not used to the bed, simply take her back to bed and firmly tell her that it's time to go to sleep and leave the room.

3. Read a story, sing a song, and give a small glass of water. If you want to help her feel independent, allow one request of her choosing, but only one, and be firm.

Starting Preschool

When your child turns three it is important for you to start looking into preschool programs.

Whether a half-day or full-day program, three times a week or five, preschool helps your child get ready for kindergarten. **Attending a high-quality program prepares your child for future academic success.**

When you are choosing a preschool—an organization that promotes quality in early education—it is important to visit the school without your child the first time. Take the time to ask questions (see below). The next time take your child with you, see how he responds to the environment, and watch how the caregivers and teachers interact with him.

Children at this age learn by observing each other. Your child will catch on to the classroom routine by watching other children take directions from the teacher and follow along.

Going to preschool helps your child socialize with other children his own age, learn to share, take turns, and build relationships.

Things to look for in a preschool:

* How is the staff interacting with the children? Is the staff engaged and excited to be working with the children? Are the expectations for the children appropriate?

* What is the teacher's experience with young children? What is the teacher's background and how does the school train their teachers?

* What does the schedule look like? Is the whole day structured and planned out? How much free play is incorporated?

Structured activities with the teacher are important. Your child's teacher should spend time with each child during structured activities to help make connections and encourage the students to socialize with other children in the class. Free time should be incorporated into the schedule as well so that your child has the opportunity to explore her own interests.

* What is the school's guidance and discipline policy? How do the caregivers handle stressful situations without losing their patience?

It is important that you follow a similar guidance and discipline policy at home so that expectations are consistent for your child. It is also crucial to see if the teacher is consistent and fair with all the children in the class.

Getting ready for preschool:

* Allow him to get his outfit for preschool ready the night before so there are no anxious last-minute battles over clothing. If your child chooses a hideous outfit, rest assured that her teacher will know that it was not your choice but your child's. Allow plenty of time to get ready each day.

* Schedule: Ask your preschool for the daily schedule ahead of time so you know what time you want to arrive and transition your child into the classroom.

* Adjust your child's sleeping schedule gradually to accommodate when he will have to wake up for school.

* Talk to your child about what he will be doing at school. Drive or walk by the preschool and point it out to your child. Ask the school if you can come for a shadow day or orientation so that your child can meet his teacher and see the classroom.

* The chances are your child won't be ready for you to just drop him off and leave on the first day, so be prepared to hang around until he's settled.

* You'll probably be feeling just as anxious and emotional as he is, but try to stay cheery and confident; children pick up on your feelings of apprehension.

* Explain to your child when you'll be back. Don't use fibs such as "Mommy's just going to move the car" when you make your exit. Tell him you'll be back after lunch time/ drink time or snack time/storytime. Leave your contact number with staff in case they need to call you.

* If your child cries and won't let you leave, ask the staff for advice. In most cases in the first few days they'll ask you to stay for a while with your child.

* When you've said your goodbyes, try not to worry. If there is a problem, you'll be contacted, but in most cases your child will be enjoying his exciting new experience.

* Remember that every child is different. Some children transition into preschool quickly, and others take more time.

Going to preschool is a time of great transition for your child. Preparing together as a family will make him more confident when the time comes.

Remember, the Whole Child Parenting Program offers appropriate developmental products and monthly activity books that walk you through supporting your child's skills. Using these in conjunction with the recommended age-appropriate room materials ensures faster development.

Safety

Your child is getting bigger and moving easily on her own. She is riding a tricycle, running, jumping, and climbing with ease.

Most injuries are preventable; they happen because parents are unaware of what their children can do. Because your child is learning so much, she is at risk for injuries from falls, burns, and even water. Your child does not remember "no" when she is exploring or playing. Stay aware of where she is and what she is doing.

Some simple guidelines for keeping your fast-moving child safe are listed here.

Electrical outlets:

Cover all electrical outlets in your home. Your three year old has a good grasp on spatial orientation and will start experimenting by sticking different objects in holes and openings to see if they fit.

Chemicals:

Keep chemicals and cleaning solutions out of reach.

Gates:

If you are letting your child explore your backyard on her own, make sure you lock any gates, especially those around pools or other unsafe areas.

Helmet:

When your child is ready to learn to ride a bike or scooter or try skates, buy her a helmet. Make sure you have one with a proper fit and one that is not too loose or too snug on the head.

Traffic and street safety:

Do not have your child play near streets, and talk to your child about not chasing any balls or toys that go into the street. **Teach your child his or her name, address, and telephone number (with area code).**

Car seats:

At this age your child still needs a car seat. Between two and three years old is a good time to change to a forward-facing car seat with a harness and tether. It is important to follow the recommended weight and height requirements for each car seat.

Playground equipment:

Before letting your child explore the playground, take a walk around the park and check the equipment to make sure it is sturdy. Keep her in sight so you can monitor how high she climbs.

Strangers:

This age is an important time to start talking about strangers. Talk to your child about what to do if someone she doesn't know approaches her. Let her know that if a stranger approaches her, she should run away yelling, immediately tell you or her caregiver, and not take anything that a stranger gives her.

Mind and Body >
Yoga

Having three year olds participate in yoga gives them the ability to exercise both their bodies and minds.

Yoga encompasses the whole child by both strengthening the body and calming the mind to shape focus and build self-confidence. Through yoga, children are able to develop and foster more than just physical skills.

Yoga helps three year olds build problem-solving skills when testing their balance. They try to move their bodies and muscles in different ways until they find the best way to achieve the position.

Yoga also helps three year olds' imagination and creativity skills. You can turn yoga into a story with your child and build language skills by having her name and sequence positions that go along with the storyline.

1. Happy Baby

Have your child lie on her back, pull her knees toward her belly, and then grab on to the outsides of her feet. Then tell her to open her knees as wide as her chest and press her feet into her hands. This pose is great for the spine, so it is important to instruct your child to keep her tailbone on the ground during this pose.

2. Butterfly Pose

This pose is great for opening the hips and a good stretch for the ankles. Remind your child to sit up straight. Pushing down on the knees or thighs with elbows as your child keeps her feet pressed together allows the hips to open up more.

3. Crescent Moon

This pose benefits the flexibility of the sides of the body. Help your child extend arms into the air and stretch fingertips off to both sides, which will cause him to balance the weight of his chest while at the same time strengthening oblique muscles and stimulating flexibility.

1. Happy
   Baby

2. Butterfly Pose

3. Crescent
   Moon

Reaching Milestones >

A three year old goes through many changes from now until she reaches the age of five. These developmental changes take place over time; no two three year olds will develop at the same pace. One three year old may reach a milestone early and another at a later time. Also, all children have a difficult week or day. Take time to observe your child a few times a week to see how she is progressing.

Use these milestones as a general guide. They are not all-inclusive. What matters most is your child's progression at a fairly steady pace. Reaching a milestone later does not mean there is a problem. It simply means she needs more time and practice to master the skills.

COGNITIVE

- Can put together simple puzzles and understand that a whole object can be separated into parts.
- Names eight colors in a crayon box (red, yellow, blue, orange, green, purple, black, brown). Can count up to five and begin to recognize written numerals 0–9.
- Can label each object with just one number word to determine the total, also known as one-to-one correspondence.
- Begins to understand time in terms of morning, night, and days of the week. Working on grasping sequence of events.
- Better able to ignore distractions and focus on task at hand. Persists in completing something that is a bit more difficult and can think more creatively when solving problems.

SOCIAL-EMOTIONAL

- Starts to play with children (as opposed to playing side by side).
- Takes turns while playing (may still need prompting by adults).
- Begins to find simple ways to solve arguments and disagreements with peers.
- Begins to be able to give comfort and show concern for a peer who is unhappy without adult prompts.
- Shows a variety of emotions beyond happy, sad, and mad (though may not name these feelings). Can better manage emotions, but may still fall apart under stress.

LANGUAGE

- Listens and understands conversations, stories, songs, and poems. Understands spatial words like *in, on, behind,* and *next*. Asks "wh" questions such as "why" to get more information.

- Turns the pages of a book one at a time. Realizes that print in books tells a reader what to say.

- Communicates in simple sentences and is refining her use of grammar. Uses five or six words in a sentence and has a two- to three-sentence conversation with others.

- Learning letters and will sometimes refer to numbers as "letters." Notices print in the environment and will ask what it means. Scribbles begin to appear more like letters and may string these "letters" along to form mock words.

- Aware of the uses for writing and may dictate to an adult to write something down.

CREATIVE

- Developing greater control over her voice and can recognize, name, and sing favorite songs.

- Plays a simple rhythm instrument with a developing ability to control beat, tempo, and pitch.

- Art begins to include recognizable subjects.

- Loves dramatic play and will get involved in her imagined scenario. Prefers real objects and costumes in her pretend play.

PHYSICAL

- Runs and walks without tripping over own feet.

- Jumps and hops on one foot.

- Kicks and throws a smaller ball; catches a smaller ball using two hands and her body.

- Starts peddling a bike and pumping a swing.

- Walks backward and climbs playground equipment.

HEALTH AND CARE

- Helps with brushing teeth.

- Puts dirty clothes in hamper independently.

- Puts on shoes without ties.

- Washes body with help.

- Puts trash in the trashcan.

- Washes and dries hands, though may need some help reaching.

Environment >
Three Year Old's Room

For three year olds the world is filled with wonder. Everywhere she looks there is something new to discover, and each discovery gives rise to learning new skills.

An environment that enhances learning excites her wonder and invites her to explore. Your home environment is full of opportunities for imagining and skill-building in the **six areas of development: cognitive, social emotional, language, creative, physical, and health.**

All children appreciate an environment that is organized, uncluttered, interesting, and attractive.

Here is a basic checklist of recommended features for your home learning environment:

1. The environment is safe for your child to explore and free from clutter.

2. The environment includes your **Six Drawer Whole Child Color-Coded Organizer** with all the materials that are appropriate for independent exploration and making choices.

3. A wall calendar/organizer is available so your child can get into a routine while using the space.

Routines include regular times for learning activities to occur. Making time for daily learning in a well-organized space will set the expectation that your child have regular learning times at home.

The following picture shows what a recommended space for a three year old's room looks like with furniture.

Whole Child: Three Year Old's Room

The following list contains must-have items for your three year old's room. These items will be used interchangeably with your other Whole Child Parenting materials.

1. Six Drawer Whole Child Color-Coded Organizer
2. Whole Child Wall Planner
3. Table and Chairs
4. Easel
5. Carpet
6. Kitchen Set
7. Bookshelf
8. Puppet/Pretend Play Materials
9. Blocks and Manipulatives

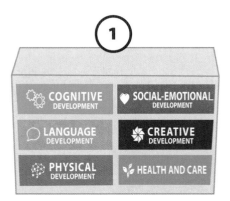

1. Six Drawer Whole Child Color-Coded Organizer

Easily organize educational materials and toys by six areas of development. Ensure your child always has enough materials in each drawer.

2. Whole Child Wall Planner

Plan and organize weekly activities based on six areas of development.

3. Table and Chairs

Provides a clearly defined space, at child's level and shaped to support posture, for child to work independently and stay focused. Use for fine motor development and learning shapes, colors, spatial concepts, science, letters, and numbers.

4. Easel

Provides a place for child to play with well-organized art materials displayed at eye level. Materials are easily changed out by child with help or by parent. Use for fostering development of child's aesthetic sense and for engaging in creative experiences.

5. Kitchen Set

Organize props and pretend food. Can be easily rotated in and out. Use to develop self-help skills, independence, and imagination.

6. Carpet

Provides a soft, safe place, free from clutter, for your child to play on. Use for providing materials in one central location at child's eye level. Enables parent to change out materials and still maintain child safety.

7. Bookshelf

Makes books easily accessible to child and supports independent exploration and literacy skills. Use for bonding with child through one-on-one time.

8. Puppet/Pretend Play Materials

Helps social communication, and interactive skills through shared experiences. Use for pretend play and peek-a-boo games.

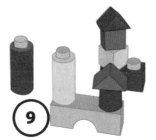

9. Blocks and Manipulatives

Used for construction and spatial skill development while talking about shapes. Helps developing recognition skills, counting, sorting and matching.

whole child activity books >

Have a look at a sample of our series of activity books for three year olds. This series of 12 titles helps three year olds exercise their brains and bodies in every category of development explored in the Whole Child Parenting books. The 12 titles are available now.

WHOLE CHILD

Age 3

Activity Book

BOAT

Transportation

WHOLE CHILD = $\dfrac{\text{smart} + \text{creative}}{\text{healthy} + \text{happy}}$

COGNITIVE
DEVELOPMENT

 Problem-solving · Attention · Numbers

SOCIAL-EMOTIONAL
DEVELOPMENT

 Self-control · Friendship · Feelings

LANGUAGE
DEVELOPMENT

 Communication · Speaking · Literacy

CREATIVE
DEVELOPMENT

 Dramatic Play · Dance · Music · Arts

PHYSICAL
DEVELOPMENT

Motor Skills: Sensory, Gross, Fine

HEALTH AND CARE

 Hygiene · Diet · Routine · Yoga

sneak peek >

COGNITIVE DEVELOPMENT

NUMBER 1

Skill • Tracing numb

Directions: Have your child look at the number 1 and say "one." Ask her
count how many trains she sees: one. Ask her to follow the arrows 1, 2, 3
trace each number 1 using a purple crayon.

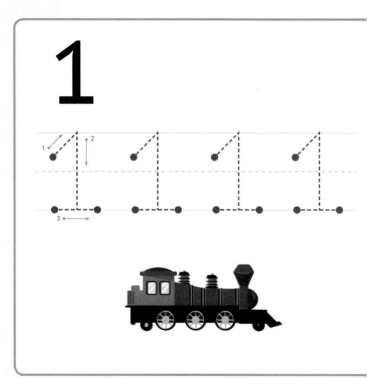

Number sense is understanding how numbers represent an amount. For examp
how the symbol "1" is related to a quantity.

8

G AND SMALL

Skill • Learning spatial concepts

ections: Ask your child to color in all of the *big* trains at the top. Have her
w a circle around all of the *small* trains at the bottom.

Learning spatial concepts big and small helps your child compare and contrast
objects based on size.

9

sneak peek >

EARLY LANGUAGE SKILLS

DISCOVER!

At three years old, you will see your child writing letters unconventionally, for example she may draw the straight line of the G before the curved line. This is because she is still developing the hand-eye coordination and fine motor skills she needs to write letters in swift motions.

DID YOU KNOW?

Tracing letters with curved lines will help your child learn how to write them without help. Sounding out simple three- to five-letter words (like the word *car*: "KUH, car") to your child helps her start to associate some letters with their letter sound.

LET'S DO MORE!

Create opportunities for your child to practice writing by having writing and drawing materials, such as crayons and pencils, easily available for her at home. Get in on the action. Sit down with your child and her box of crayons and write her a message, fold it up, and deliver it to her as a surprise. You can then read "her mail" together.

URVED LINES

Skill • Tracing lines

ections: Have your child start at the black dot and trace the four curved
es using a green crayon.

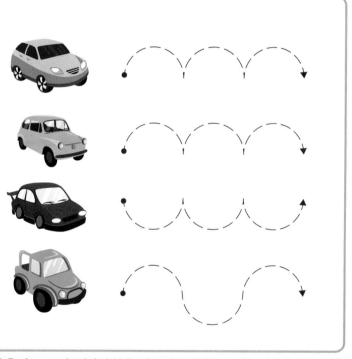

Tracing curved and straight lines is an important pre-writing skill that your child
will need to master until she can fashion the letters on her own.

sneak peek >

CREATIVE
DEVELOPMENT

COLORING
Skill • Developing creativi

Directions: Have your child color the plane using red, yellow, and blue crayo
Ask him to practice coloring inside the lines.

By experimenting with the three primary colors, your child is exploring the outco
of mixing colors together.

TTLE PLANES Skill • Rhyming

rections: Read the rhyme to your child. Have him practice being a plane
d landing on a runway.

*Three little airplanes flying in the sky
come in for a landing from way up high.
The first little airplane shining in the sun
landed on runway number 1.*

*The second little
airplane carrying
its crew
landed on runway
number 2.*

*The third little airplane,
such a sight to see,
landed on runway
number 3.*

The words and rhymes give clues about what new rhyming words might follow,
for example, sun-1, crew-2, see-3.

sneak peek >

whole child parenting program >

Get a sneak peek into the next Whole Child Parenting book. ***Whole Child Parenting: Age Four*** is a comprehensive look into your four year old's development. The book is available now.

WHOLE CHILD
PARENTING

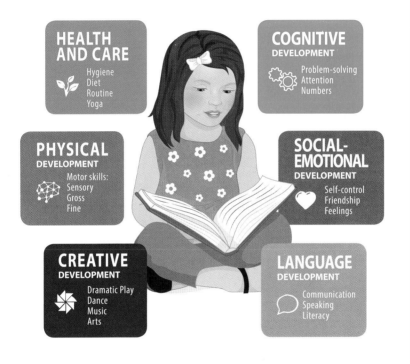

HEALTH AND CARE
Hygiene
Diet
Routine
Yoga

COGNITIVE DEVELOPMENT
Problem-solving
Attention
Numbers

PHYSICAL DEVELOPMENT
Motor skills:
Sensory
Gross
Fine

SOCIAL-EMOTIONAL DEVELOPMENT
Self-control
Friendship
Feelings

CREATIVE DEVELOPMENT
Dramatic Play
Dance
Music
Arts

LANGUAGE DEVELOPMENT
Communication
Speaking
Literacy

AGE FOUR

Parents, educators, and caregivers
will learn how best to encourage growth and
skill-building in all six developmental areas.

sneak peek >

Milestones for a Four Year Old

COGNITIVE 1

- Focuses attention more
- Uses five senses to learn math concepts
- Uses spatial language
- Uses problem-solving skills
- Memory and recall improve

 SOCIAL-EMOTIONAL 2

- Builds strong peer ties
- Uses language to express feelings and thoughts
- Controls emotions better
- Develops positive self-esteem and self-identity

 LANGUAGE 3

- Attention span increases
- Understands and comprehends meanings
- Uses around 1,500 words
- Gains phonetic knowledge and writing skills

 CREATIVE

- Creates music and responds to music patterns
- Creates and invents new forms of art
- Dances and performs other body movements

PHYSICAL 5

- Hand-eye coordination skills develop
- Uses senses to guide locomotion
- Balance and endurance increase

 HEALTH AND CARE 6

- Better understands healthful lifestyles
- Is independent with self-help skills
- Understands some other cultures

four

Welcome to age four! This is a year with great changes in your child's growing independence as well as in your relationship with your child. This year will bring more than just problem solving but also reasoning skills and curiosity. Age four is a great time to start communicating openly and comfortably with your child about all the questions and concerns he can articulate about himself and his environment and those in it.

sneak peek >

1. Cognitive Development

> **Cognitive development refers to the building of thinking methods, which includes how your child will remember, problem solve, and make decisions from now and into adulthood.**

At age four your child is now able to focus his attention more accurately and is less influenced by distractions, which is important because it will enable him to complete and engage in more challenging tasks. The eagerness to ask questions increases as your child develops a strong curiosity about the world around him.

By this age, your child will have increased memory, which accounts for a big part of his learning capability. This increase in memory supports your child in retaining more and different information at the same time.

Cognitive development at this age includes your child learning more about cause and effect as well as similarities and differences through everyday activities. Cognitive skills are at the forefront of your child's ability to process information, pay attention, memorize, and perform many other learning tasks.

The following chart provides you with an image that walks you through your child's stages of intellectual development.

Understanding these areas of cognitive development will help you learn how your child thinks, how to support learning, and how to teach new skills.

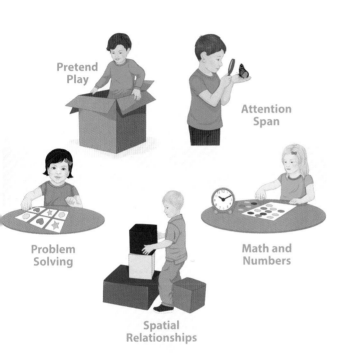

Pretend
Play

Attention
Span

Problem
Solving

Math and
Numbers

Spatial
Relationships

WHOLE CHILD: AGE FOUR
Cognitive
Development Components

sneak peek >

Attention Span >
Concentration and Focus

Attention span involves the amount of time your child is able to concentrate and focus on a single activity.

If your child fails to develop strong attention skills, she will have problems with everything from math to social relationships.

Your child now has the ability to focus her attention more accurately and will be less influenced by distractions going on around her, which is important because this will enable her to engage in and complete more challenging tasks later on.

ACTIVITY

Sam and Mom are sitting a the table. Mom pulls out one of Sam's favorite memor games. "Are you ready to play Anima Memory?" says Mom. "Yes, I am!" Sam takes out the 12 game tiles, flips them a over face down, scrambles them up, and arranges them into a grid. Sam goes first by flipping over two tiles at a time. "Aw, got a zebra and an elephant," Sam says "It's your turn, Mom!" Her eyes wander to her electronic tablet. Mom takes her turn and gets a zebra and a goat. "Sam over here, it's your turn!" says Mom. Sam proceeds to turn over a tile; the first one she gets is a lion. She pauses for a moment, then turns over another tile getting a giraffe. "Sam, did you notice what my tiles were?" says Mom. Sam says, "Zebra and . . . elephant?"

Left brain activities to do with your child to develop attention skills:

1. This is the first and most important activity to do. Change your child's diet by reducing sugar, increasing raw vegetables and fruit, using fewer processed foods, and increasing the amount of water your child drinks. A simple change of the diet makes a tremendous difference in your child's attention span.

2. Take five to 10 minutes each day to listen to music such as Mozart and Putumayo's *World Sing Along*. Talk about one instrument in the music (for example, piano or drums); this will require your child to pay attention and listen for the instrument. You may ask, "Did you hear the drums play fast or slowly?"

3. Play a game once a week of stacking blocks, then build in another day the following week, and continue till you are doing building projects a bunch of times a week. You would start this game by gathering six blocks, stack them any way you like, and then have your child copy you. This will require focus and attention to stack the blocks like yours.

INSIGHT

During this game Sam is not paying close attention to what tiles are being revealed and placed back down by Mom. Mom even has to remind Sam that it is now her turn to play. It is actually not unusual for Sam to lose attention at her age. She is still learning to focus her attention on a task for longer periods of time. Memory games are a great way for Sam to exercise her brain by improving her concentration, focus, and visual memory skills while increasing her attention span. As Sam grows older and the two of them play more memory games, she will become better and better at using her new skills in other areas of his development, such as in math.

Whole Child Parenting: Age Four
Available now >

WHOLE CHILD

Parenting Program books and materials
are available worldwide.

Birth to Age Five

Parents, educators, and caregivers
will learn how best to encourage growth and
skill-building in all six developmental areas.

*The book that
kick started the
program!*

Also available separately

INFANT
(Birth to 12 Months)

Parents, educators, and caregivers
will learn how best to encourage growth and
skill-building in all six developmental areas.

TODDLER
(12 to 24 Months)

Parents, educators, and caregivers
will learn how best to encourage growth and
skill-building in all six developmental areas.

AGE TWO

Parents, educators, and caregivers
will learn how best to encourage growth and
skill-building in all six developmental areas.

AGE THREE

Parents, educators, and caregivers
will learn how best to encourage growth and
skill-building in all six developmental areas.

AGE FOUR

Parents, educators, and caregivers
will learn how best to encourage growth and
skill-building in all six developmental areas.

Whole Child
Program
Activity Books

- 4 **Infant** Titles
- 6 **Toddler** Titles
- 12 **Age Two** Titles
- 12 **Age Three** Titles
- 12 **Age Four** Titles

Whole Child Program books and materials are available at
special discounts when purchased in bulk for premiums and
sales promotions as well as for fundraising or educational use.
For details, please contact us at: sales@wholechild.co

Visit us on the web at: www.wholechild.co